The Book Of Mary

The Book Of Mary

Second Edition
Michael P. Closs

ARPress
ILLUMINATING IDEAS,
EMPOWERING VOICES

ARPress
45 Dan Road Suite 15
Canton MA 02021

Hotline: 1(888) 821-0229
Fax: 1(508) 545-7580

Ordering Information:
Quantity sales. Special discounts are available on quantity purchases by corporations, associations, and others. For details, contact the publisher at the address above.

Printed in the United States of America.

ISBN-13:	Softcover	979-8-89356-827-1
	Hardcover	979-8-89676-084-9
	eBook	979-8-89356-828-8

Library of Congress Control Number: 2024907666

Contents

Introduction to the Second Edition

The Book of Mary, 2016[1], provided an English translation and commentary on the *Protevangelium of James*, briefly referred to here as the 'Protevangelium', that is, 'Before the Gospels'.

The translation of the Protevangelium is derived from the work of Émile Amann which was published in 1910.[2] My publication was a critique of Amann's commentary, just as his was a critique of the critical edition published by C. von Tischendorf that resulted from his study of seventeen manuscripts in 1853, and later republished in 1876.[3] The Tischendorf edition, quickly became the most important source for the interpretation of the Protevangelium in the western world. His analysis had important consequences for the western Catholic understanding of the Protevangelium which had previously been based on the work of ancient Greek commentators. Amann was 'commissioned' by ecclesiastical officials to evaluate Tischendorf's work. His publication had a major impact because he was familiar with the work of Greek and Latin commentators, and he also had access to a 5th century Syriac manuscript that was far older than any of the manuscripts that Tischendorf had used. Amann's commentary included helpful insights into the Protevangelium but, in the end, I found his work seriously flawed.

In Closs, 2016, I introduced an English translation of Amann's French text of the Protevangelium and my own commentary on his commentary. I also introduced a number of novel implications concerning the contents of the Protevangelium and suggested alternative approaches in evaluating them. The results had important implications for Tischendorf's original analysis.

Amann's work had an impact among western Catholic scholars at the time of its publication and essentially marginalized the Protevangelium in the western tradition for over a century despite the fact that it had been regarded as the source of a number of teachings on Mary that took root in the early apostolic churches.

Roland F. Hock[4] noted that the Tischendorf edition had become the 'textus receptus' for translations of the *Protevangelium of James* and this endured for over a century. An English translation of the Protevangelium in 1993 by J. K. Elliott[5] and a later extension of that work was published in a new printing, Elliott and Rumsey, 2022[6]. These were also based on Tischendorf and were updates of an earlier translation by M. R. James.[7] Elliott did not significantly change the basic consensus established by the work of Tischendorf. It may also be noted that Elliott, 1993, and Hock, 1995, were focused only on Greek manuscripts of the Protevangelium. This is a

---

[1] Closs, Michael P. *The Book of Mary, A Commentary on the Protevangelium of James*. Friesen Press, Victoria, Canada, 2016.
[2] Amann, Émile. *Le Protévangile de Jacques et Ses Remaniements Latins*. Paris, 1910.
[3] Tischendorf, C. (ed.), *Evangelia Apocrypha. Leipzig*: Avenarius and Mendelssohn, 2nd edition, 1876, 1–50.
[4] Hock, Roland F. *The Infancy Gospels of James and Thomas*. Santa Rosa, California, 1995.
[5] Elliott, J. K. *Apocryphal New Testament: A Collection of Apocryphal Christian Literature in an English Translation*. Oxford: Clarendon Press, 1993.
[6] Elliott, J. K. (introduction, editor, and translation) and Rumsey, Patrica M. (commentary). *The Protevangelium of James*. Brepols, Turnhout, Belgium. 2022.
[7] James, M. R. *The Apocryphal New Testament: A Collection of Apocryphal Christian Literature in an English Translation*. Oxford University Press, 1924.

major handicap because it ignored the Syriac manuscript, which for a long time had been the oldest copy of the Protevangelium in the world.

Elliott and Rumsey, 2022:39, suggest that the Protevangelium was composed originally in Greek but is a work of Syrian origins and cite the enormous favour it enjoyed within the Syrian Christian communities and a number of specific ties it shared with ancient Syriac sources. They conclude that it was very likely composed in Syria. This underlies the importance that was placed on the Syriac text used by Amann in his critique of Tischendorf.

A major addition to the inventory on the Protevangelium was the early-fourth-century Papyrus Bodmer V, discovered in Egypt in 1952. It was studied by Émile de Strycker, who published a French version and commentary in1961.[8] Hock, 1995, in his discussion on the Protevangelium included copies of the text and drew on de Stryker's work. His work was also informed by the commentary of H. R. Smid.[9]

Recently, George Themilios Zervos has published a new critical edition of the Greek text of the Protevangelium.[10] He also suggested that the Protevangelium 'may be assigned to the first century CE with the canonical Gospels' (Zervos, 2021:197).

Closs, 2016, had focused on a century old problem related to Tischendorf and Amann's critique of it. Hock also suggested that at the present time, most scholars accepted the late second century as the most likely date for the Protevangelium. Nevertheless, he also indicated other materials that suggested a possible earlier date. Elliott and Rumsey, 2022, also commented on other earlier indicators, as did Closs, 2016. In that edition, I tentatively dated the Protevangelium to the end of the first century and beginning of the second century. Of particular interest was an association with Revelation 11:19–12:5 (Closs, 2016: 197-200). This suggested it may have been in existence at about 95 CE and fell within the period of the latest canonical Christian scriptures. This raised many questions. The Gospel of John is also conventionally dated to about the same time as Revelation. Other questions arose pertaining to the temporal relationship of the Protevangelium with other canonical sources. Research on this problem led me to Closs, 2025.

It uses the translation developed in Closs, 2016, with some minor amendments, based on the work of Amann, and follows the chapter settings first instituted by J. A. Fabricius.[11]. Its versification is for the most part the same as that used in the original edition. The new commentary also draws on several concepts that have been previously mentioned but adds much new information and modifies some earlier comments. Importantly, it also adopts a new interpretive framework that differs from Closs, 2016, and from that used in all other western commentators studying the Protevangelium. I have reduced my citations to Amann, ignoring statements that I no longer consider helpful, but have maintained several of them because for over a century Amann's study did have access to what had been the oldest manuscript of the Protevangelium in existence. His translation appears to have been ignored by many of the most recent commentators. The Syriac manuscript influenced his

---

[8] de Strycker, Émile. *La forme la plus ancienne du Protévangile de Jacques* (Brussels, 1961).
[9] Smid, H. R. *Protevangelium Jacobi: A Commentary*. Assen, 1965.
[10] Zervos, George Themelios. *The Protevangelium of James, Greek text, English Translation, Critical Introduction, Volume 1*. T & T Clark, Bloomsbury Publishing, 2019 (paperback edition, 2021).
[11] Fabricius, J. A. *Codex Apocryphus Novi Testamenti*, 4 vols. Hamburg, 1719.

translation on several points and such information should not be lost because it is more up to date then all of the previous commentators that have been published until the discovery of Bodmer V. The Syriac manuscript is now the second oldest manuscript in the world, but more recently it has been suggested that an 'original' edition appears to have been published in Syria. As a result, the Syriac manuscript is likely to be the most authentic version of the original manuscript in the world.

Biblical quotes – unless specifically noted to the contrary – follow the New Revised Standard Version (NRSV), Catholic Edition. I have also used The New Jerusalem Bible (NJB) and on occasion NETS, A New English Translation of the Septuagint, 2007.

The Messianic Secret in the Gospel of Mark

The Gospel of Mark was written between 65–70 CE. The concept of the messianic secret in the Gospel of Mark was first proposed by William Wrede in 1901 and has been the subject of much discussion.[12] The gospel itself is set in the period lying between 30–33 CE with the latter date marking the death of Jesus. It is the most secure date in any chronology that concerns Jesus. As a result, the gospel was written more than 30 years after the death of Jesus, but its narrative setting is more than thirty years earlier.

The gospel begins with a brief initial statement: 'The beginning of the good news of Jesus Christ, the Son of God'. (Mark 1:1). A footnote observes that 'other ancient authorities lack the Son of God'. This implies that this title is not in what are believed to be the earliest records of Mark's gospel and scholars accept that its presence here is a late development.

The gospel continues with the proclamation of John the Baptist which focuses on 'a baptism of repentance for the forgiveness of sins' (Mark 1:4). It was in these days that Jesus came from Nazareth and was baptized by John in the Jordan.

> Antiphon. And just as he was coming out of the water, he saw the heavens torn apart and the Spirit descending like a dove on him. And a voice came from heaven, "You are my Son, the Beloved; with you I am well pleased." (Mark 1:10–11).

The Spirit descending from heaven like a dove on Jesus is an anointing (Heb. 'messiah') and the voice from heaven also describes Jesus as the 'Son of God'.

Those reading Mark's gospel are Christians and would understand that the Spirit anointed Jesus as the Messiah and that the title 'Son of God' refers to the divine status of Jesus. These beliefs were already accepted in professions of faith as shown in Romans 8:3–4, Philippians 2:5–1 and Hebrews 1:1–3 that were written after the death of Jesus but before the Gospel of Mark.

If one returns to the gospel setting, some 30 years earlier, people were not aware of Jesus' baptism. The description in Mark does not indicate that anyone else is present at the baptism and there is no indication that John the Baptist ever talked about it. Those present during Jesus' public ministry – dating from the baptism of Jesus to his death – were not aware of it. The baptism of Jesus is the first use of the idea of the 'messianic secret'. The event had happened but nobody would be aware of it; they would not know he was the Messiah nor did they understand that he was the Son of God in a sense that attested to his divine status.

The secret also shows up dramatically in two other incidents in the gospel. On a journey to Caesarea Philippi, Jesus asked his disciples. 'Who do people say that I am?' It was a question that pertained to his identity. They gave a variety of answers, and then Jesus spoke to his disciples.

---

[12] Wrede, William. *Das Messiasgeheimnis in den Evangelium: Zugleich ein Beitrag zum Verständis des Markusevangelium.* Göttingen: Vandenhoeck & Ruprecht, 1901; English edition, *William Wrede, The Messianic Secret.* Trans. The Rev'd James C. G. Grieg. Cambridge: James Clarke & Co., 1971). See also, Wikipedia, 'messianic secret'.

Antiphon. He asked them, 'But who do you say that I am?' Peter answered him, 'You are the Messiah.' And he sternly ordered them to not tell anyone about him. (Mark 8:29–30).

Jesus had decided that he did not want people to know who he was. Then, Jesus began to teach his disciples that the 'Son of Man' – a title used by Jesus that emphasized his human status – would be killed and rise again after three days. 'He said all this quite openly' (Mark 8:31–32).

A week after this, he took Peter, James, and John and led them on another journey.

Antiphon. Six days later, Jesus took with him Peter and James and John, and led them up to a high mountain apart, by themselves. And he was transfigured before them, and his clothes became dazzling white, such as no one on earth could bleach them. And there appeared to them Elijah with Moses, who were talking with Jesus. … Then a cloud overshadowed them, and from the cloud there came a voice, 'This is my Son, the Beloved; listen to him.' (Mark 9:2–4, 7).

As they were coming down the mountain, he ordered them to tell no one about what had happened until after the Son of Man had risen from the dead (Mark 9:9).

The two episodes show that Jesus spoke of the messianic secret concerning his identification of being the Messiah and of being the 'Son of God'. This information was used by Mark to implement the 'messianic secret' in his development of the narrative structure of the gospel. There are other instances in Mark where the secret is explicitly mentioned by Jesus.

Returning to the beginning of the Gospel of Mark, immediately after the baptism of Jesus, the Spirit drove him 'out into the wilderness' and he was there 'for forty days, tempted by Satan' (Mark 1:12– 13). No information on the temptation is given, but Mark is making a different point. Although people did not know about the baptism, evil spirits did. They were aware of his anointing by the Spirit and of the voice that came from heaven, because the baptism itself is a public event. Although other people did not see it, the phenomena accompanying the baptism would be discernible to Satan.

It was 'after John was arrested' that 'Jesus came to Galilee, to proclaim the good news of God, and to teach that 'the time is fulfilled, and the kingdom of God has come near' (Mark 1:14–15). It is the dawn of the messianic age.

Jesus was teaching in the synagogue at Capernaum, and 'a man with an unclean spirit' cried out, 'What have you to do with us, Jesus of Nazareth? Have you come to destroy us? I know who you are, the Holy One of God.' But Jesus rebuked him, saying, 'Be silent, and come out of him!' And the unclean spirit, throwing him into convulsions came out of him. (Mark 1:23–25).

The incident is early in the gospel and there is something singular about it. One question arises in the terminology of Mark for he used the expression 'unclean spirit'. And, it is also said that people were amazed that Jesus 'commands even the unclean spirits, and they obey him' (Mark 1:27). There is something else about this episode because although Jesus silenced the unclean spirit, it still managed to identify Jesus with a title about his identity. The unclean spirit had been silenced by the messianic secret and the implication is that any human who heard the message would also be silenced about it.

Later that evening – again important because of its early appearance in the gospel – people were brought to Jesus 'all who were sick or possessed with demons'.

> Antiphon. And he cured many who were sick with various diseases, and cast out many demons; and he would not permit the demons to speak, because they knew him. (Mark 1:34).

This introduces us to two features in Jesus' ministry including cures for the sick and casting out demons. It also affirms that Jesus says that the demons 'knew him'.

Readers of Mark's gospel, more than 30 years after the death of Jesus, are assured that the earlier title about Jesus' identity revealed by the unclean spirit has been approved by Jesus as legitimate. Mark wants the reader of the gospel to know this. This is a part of a code that Mark is using.

Now, consider a few cures of Jesus to see how they relate to the messianic secret.

> Antiphon. A leper came to him begging him, and kneeling he said to him, 'If you choose, you can make me clean.' Moved with pity, Jesus stretched out his hand and touched him, and said to him, 'I do choose. Be made clean! Immediately the leprosy left him, and he was made clean. After sternly warning him he sent him away at once, saying to him, 'See that you say nothing to anyone; but go, show yourself to the priest, and offer for your cleansing what Moses commanded as a testimony to them. (Mark 1:40–44).

Unfortunately, the cured man went out and spread what had happened and proclaimed it freely although he had received a stern warning to 'say nothing to anyone'. A consequence of this was that Jesus 'stretched out his hand and touched the leper'. As a result, people would think he was unclean, and he could no longer go into the town and had to stay out in the country.

> Antiphon. They brought to him a deaf man who had an impediment in his speech; and they begged him to lay his hand on him. He took him aside in private, away from the crowd, and put his fingers into his ears, and he spat and touched his tongue. Then looking up to heaven, he sighed and said to him, 'Ephphatha', that is, 'Be opened.' And immediately his ears were opened, his tongue was released, and he spoke plainly, Then Jesus ordered them to tell no one: but the more he ordered them, the more zealously they proclaimed it. (Mark 7:32–36).

In these two examples, Jesus ordered the cures he worked to be kept quiet, but the people involved did not listen to him. Jesus may compel demons to be silent and those who heard them to be silent, but he does not compel people who are receiving cures in the same way. They will be silent only through an exercise of their own will. They are free to listen to him or to not listen to him.

It is also apparent that in many cures, Jesus acts spontaneously, and although witnesses may be present, he is not fearful to act, and there are no indications in these situations that he was asking for silence.

With respect to the casting out of demons, there is a standard rule that Jesus silences them. However, one unusual instance of an unclean spirit actually provided a title for Jesus that concerned his identity, and it was registered in the gospel. There are two other examples in the gospel of such things happening with unclean spirits.

> Antiphon. Whenever the unclean spirits saw him [Jesus] they fell down before him and shouted, 'You are the Son of God!' But he sternly ordered them not to make him known. (Mark 3:11–12).

> Antiphon. And when he had stepped out of the boat, immediately a man out of the tombs with an unclean spirit met him. … When he saw Jesus from a distance, he ran and bowed down before him; 'What have you to do with me, Jesus, Son of the Most High God? I adjure you by God do not torment me.' For he had said to him, 'come out of the man, you unclean spirit!' (Mark 5:2, 6–8).

There are three titles of Jesus issued by unclean spirits in Mark's gospel that identify him in some respect.

> Jesus, Holy One of God (Mark 1:23–25)
> Jesus, Son of God (Mark 3:11–12)
> Jesus, Son of the Most High God (Mark 5:2,6–8)

In each case, the unclean spirits were silenced and anyone who heard these titles would also have been silenced. Yet, those reading Mark's gospel – long after the death of Jesus – saw the titles and accepted them as authentic. This is a puzzle. Where did the titles come from? One can rule out the canonical scriptures in the New Testament for these titles occur in the public ministry and the New Testament did not exist and would not for many years. Then, one must look back in time before the baptism of Jesus, around 30 CE, the time when Mark used the messianic secret as a convention in his narrative.

Before studying the problem, it is important to look at Mark's use of the term 'unclean spirit' and to understand why people were amazed that Jesus could remove them from Israel. The answer is in a messianic text of the prophet Zechariah, dated 520–518 BCE.

> Antiphon. On that day a fountain shall be opened for the house of David and the inhabitants of Jerusalem, to cleanse them from sin and impurity. On that day says the Lord of hosts, I will cut off the names of the idols from the land, so that they shall be remembered no more; and also I will remove from the land the prophets and the unclean spirit. (Zechariah 13:1–2).

Zechariah is speaking of the opening of the messianic age when the 'unclean spirit' will be removed from Israel. Some 500 years later, Jesus is now expelling unclean spirits from Israel at the dawn of the messianic age. It is these unclean spirits who produce the three titles for Jesus in the Gospel of Mark.

The 'prophets' in the Zechariah citation refer to false prophets that are discredited by their abuses (Jeremiah 23:9–32; Ezekiel 13). The cleansing from the fountain is also described by Ezekiel: 'I shall pour clean water over you and you will be cleansed; I shall cleanse you of all your filth and of all your foul idols (Ezekiel 36:25). The notion is also expressed in a messianic poem attributed to Isaiah that people 'with joy will draw water from the wells of salvation' (Isaiah 12:3). Isaiah, looked ahead to the messianic age when the ears of the deaf were unstopped – see Mark 7:32–36 that has been discussed above – and other miracles that were to take place. He observed that, 'waters shall break forth in the wilderness, and streams in the desert; the burning sand shall become a pool, and the thirsty ground springs of water' (Isaiah 35:5–7).

The theological background for the messianic age is found in the teachings of Isaiah, dated 740–686 BCE and Ezekiel, dated 592–570 BCE. They are both priests and prophets of the temple and their teachings have a priestly focus and are shaped by ancient laws concerning what is clean and unclean and the law of holiness.

The 'law of purity' (Leviticus 11–16) involves religious taboos of great antiquity. What is 'clean' is considered worthy to approach God; what is 'unclean' makes a person unfit for ritual worship or excludes a person from it. This legislation establishes an ideal of moral purity, safeguarded by positive observances. (Leviticus 11:1, fn. a. NJB).

The 'law of holiness' (Leviticus 17–26) complements the 'law of purity'. It is the positive aspect of a divine demand whereas the law of purity is a negative aspect. The form of the law of holiness is priestly as it comes down to us. The basic elements appear to date from the end of the monarchical period and represents the usages of the temple in Jerusalem. There are evident points of contact between it and the thought of Ezekial, which also seems to be the product of a pre-exilic movement. Holiness is one of the essential attributes of the God of Israel (Leviticus, 17:1, fn. a. NJB).

For I am the Lord your God; sanctify yourselves therefore, and be holy for I am holy (Leviticus 11:44).

The Book of Isaiah is divided into three successive portions: Isaiah = First Isaiah, chs. 1 39, dated 740 686 BCE; Second-Isaiah, chs. 40–55, dated to 6th century BCE, written during the Exile; and Third-Isaiah, chs. 56–66, composed after the return from the Exile. Third-Isaiah is a collection of work of the disciples of Second-Isaiah and possibly a deliberate re-interpretation of his work. It is the final product of the Isaian tradition.

The central focus in the messianic messages of Isaiah is concerned with holiness. Isaiah is responsible for the great messianic hymn that describes in detail salient characteristics of the coming Messiah in Isaiah 11:1–9. The earliest of the messianic titles emanating from unclean spirits is 'Holy One of God' and the Lord is the unique Holy One. Isaiah often uses the title 'Holy One of Israel' to refer to the Lord. Of the 29 uses of 'Holy One of Israel' in the Old Testament, 24 of them are in Isaiah. Isaiah also refers to God directly as the 'Holy One' and of eight occurrences in the Old Testament, four of them are in Isaiah.

The specific messianic title 'Holy One of God' applied to Jesus indicates that Jesus is the Holy One of God and asserts his divine status. The title appears to be in the Isaian tradition, but no such title exists there.

The second of the messianic titles from unclean spirits is 'Son of God'. The term 'son of God' is used in the Old Testament in biblical references where it does not imply a natural sonship but a sonship that is adoptive. It indicates God's deliberate choice to set up an intimate relationship between God and his creatures. It is given to heavenly beings [Hebrew: *sons of God*] (Job 1:6, Psalm 82:6) and to Israel (Exodus 4:22, Hosea 11:1). An extension is given to Israel as 'children of God' (Deuteronomy 14:1) or as 'daughter of God' (Hosea 2).

This love extends to all humanity. 'As a father has compassion for his children, so the Lord has compassion for those who fear him. For he knows how we were made; he remembers that we are dust' (Psalm 103:13–14). 'The Lord has established his throne in the heavens, and his kingdom extends over all (Psalm 103:19).

The title 'son of God', however, is also involved in the Hebrew concept of a royal Messiah. This is derived from the covenant that the Lord made with David through the prophet Nathan.[13]

> Antiphon. When your days are fulfilled and you lie down with your ancestors, I will raise up your offspring after you, who shall come forth from your body, and I will establish his kingdom. He shall build a house for my name, and I will establish the throne of his kingdom for ever. I will be a father to him, and he shall be a son to me. When he commits iniquity, I will punish him with a rod such as mortals use, with blows inflicted by human beings. But I will not take my steadfast love from him, as I took it from Saul, whom I put away from before you. Your house and your kingdom shall be made sure for ever before me; your throne shall be established for ever. (2 Samuel 7:12– 16).

Other prophecies related to the Davidic Messiah appear in Micah 4:14–5:1; Haggai 2:23; and Psalms 2, 45, 72, 89 and 110.

The title 'son of God' is assigned to the Davidic Messiah when the Lord says: 'I will be a father to him and he shall be a son to me'. The possibility of assigning this as a reference to Jesus in Mark is not acceptable because of the messianic secret since a variation of the title 'You are my Son, the Beloved' had been used at the baptism of Jesus.

The third title given to Jesus by an unclean spirit is 'Son of the Most High God'. The most relevant episode in the Old Testament concerns the story of Abram's meeting with Melchizedek in Genesis 14:17–24. This occurs shortly before the Lord made a covenant with Abram and changed his name to Abraham (Genesis 15–17).

Abram and his allies had been engaged in a great battle with enemy kings and – after a triumph – he was returning home. The king of Sodom came to meet him in the Valley of Shaveh (that is, the King's Valley). And King Melchizedek of Salem – recognized in subsequent Jewish tradition as Jerusalem (see Psalm 76:2) – brought out bread and wine. He was priest of God Most High (Heb. *El Elyon*). He blessed him and said, 'Blessed be Abram by God Most High, maker of heaven and earth; and blessed be God Most High, who has delivered your

---

[13] 2 Samuel:7, fn. a, NJB. The substance of the prophecy is the perpetuity of the Davidic dynasty in Israel. And so, David himself understood it, vv.19, 25, 27, 29. The prophecy stretches beyond Solomon, David's immediate successor to whom it is applied. There is an interplay of light and shade in the prophecy, however, and it allows us a glimpse of one privileged descendant who is to enjoy God's special favour. It is the first in the series of prophecies relating to the Davidic Messiah (Isaiah 7:14f, 9:1–6, 11:1–9.

enemies into your hand!' And Abram gave him one tenth of everything. (Genesis:17–20). The tithe of Abram shows that Melchizedek had a status greater than that of Abram.

Then the king of Sodom said to Abram, 'Give me the people, but take the goods for yourself.' But Abram said to the King of Sodom, 'I have sworn to the Lord, God Most High, maker of heaven and earth' that I would not take a thread or a sandal-thong, or anything that is yours, so that you might not say, "I have made Abram rich." (Genesis 14:21–23).

Abram then swears an oath using the name of the Lord (Yahweh) and the name of God Most High, maker of heaven and earth. In doing so, he identifies the two as the God whom Abram worships. In this context then, the Lord = God Most High. In consequence, the title 'Son of God', explored previously, and the title 'Son of the Most High God' are equivalent. The equality is a historical result, and the titles are equivalent without regard to the messianic secret.

As before, in the case of the title 'Son of God' there is no reason to accept that the title 'Son of the Most High God' can be assigned to Jesus in Mark because of the messianic secret. Since both titles are equivalent then they are equally banished by the messianic secret.

Since all three titles from the unclean spirits – after examining the most relevant sources in the Old Testament – cannot be used because of the messianic secret then the mystery remains. Where did they come from?

There are two brief historical messages concerning Jesus in Mark that are useful to examine. Near the beginning of his public ministry, Jesus visited Nazareth, his hometown, and taught in the local synagogue. This is an important moment because it gives Mark the opportunity to say something of the identity of Jesus.

> Antiphon. He left that place and came to his home town, and his disciples followed him. On the sabbath he began to teach in the synagogue, and many who heard him were astounded. They said, 'Where did this man get get all this? What is this wisdom that has been given to him? What deeds of power are being done by his hands! Is not this the carpenter, the son of Mary and brother of James and Joses and Judas and Simon, and are not his sisters here with us?' And they took offence at him. (Mark 6:1–3).

In Nazareth, Jesus is teaching in the synagogue 'in the spirit of wisdom and understanding, the spirit of counsel and might, the spirit of knowledge and the fear of the Lord' (Isaiah 11:2), yet the people turn against him. With respect to the family of Jesus, Mark provides minimum but valuable information for he informs the reader that Jesus is 'the carpenter, the son of Mary'. This is the first direct information about the identity of Jesus, and one now knows that Mary is the mother of Jesus. Joseph is not mentioned or discussed, almost certainly because he was dead. All the brothers and sisters of Jesus are then related directly to Jesus and are not associated with Mary. Mary knows about the birth of Jesus but it is privileged information. She cannot reveal what she knows because it would be harmful to Jesus. This is an extension of the messianic secret in the special case of Mary. Jesus did not want the secret that he was the Messiah to come out and it included Mary. In such a case, she is unable to share what she knows with other family members.

Another important episode in Mark, concerns a situation in which Jesus is teaching in the temple, and he gives the first hint concerning his role as Messiah.

> Antiphon. While Jesus was teaching in the temple, he said, 'How can the scribes say that the Messiah is the son of David?' David himself, by the Holy Spirit, declared, "The Lord said to my Lord, 'Sit at my right hand, until I put your enemies under your feet.' " David himself calls him Lord; so how can he be his son?' And the large crowd was listening to him with delight. (Mark 12:35–37).

Jesus is discussing Psalm 110, a messianic psalm, and raised an interesting question about it. For readers of Mark, who recognized Jesus as the Messiah, his divine status was not a problem. For the ones present to the moment, some 30 years earlier, Jesus suggested that the psalm needed to be better understood. If they did so, they would encounter the statement: The Lord has sworn and will not change his mind, 'You are a priest for ever according to the order of Melchizadek,' (Psalm 110:4). The text indicates that the Messiah would also have a divine status as 'priest for ever' that went beyond the Levitical priesthood assumed by David. It raised the question that the Messiah was more than just a descendant of David but someone to whom David himself could refer to as 'Lord'. Given the large crowd and the curiosity about Jesus there would be priests – or their informers there – who would pay attention to this comment and study it. The priests who are involved in understanding what is going on would take this comment with great interest. There are problems with the Davidic Messiah wherein one must mediate between a fully human Messiah and a Messiah who will reign for ever. Jesus is suggesting a solution for them based on one of the messianic psalms.

Melchizedek's brief and mysterious appearance in the narrative as king of Jerusalem and priest of God Most High is localized since Jerusalem is the location where Yahweh will choose to dwell long before the Levitical priesthood was established. Psalm 110:4 shows Melchizedek as a figure of David, who later will be a king of Jerusalem and priest of Yahweh, but whose descendant will be the Messiah, king of Jerusalem, and priest of God Most High for ever.

It is only at the end of his ministry, shortly before his death, that Jesus publicly reveals that he is the Messiah. This occurred during his trial in which the 'high priest' and 'all the chief priests, the elders, and the scribes' had been called to assemble. After hearing the dissension in the reports of the witnesses that had been called, the high priest stood up and asked Jesus, 'Have you no answer? What is it that they testify against you?' But he was silent and did not answer. Then, the high priest, using the power of his office, turned to Jesus and directly asked the key question, 'Are you the Messiah, the Son of the Blessed One?' These are the two key titles that have been hidden by the messianic secret. Jesus replied, 'I am', a response that invoked the name of God. Jesus did not stop with the simple acceptance of the charge against him but he amplified it with two additional messianic prophesies, 'you will see the Son of Man seated at the right hand of the Power', and 'coming with the clouds of heaven'. (Mark 14:60–63)[14].

---

[14] The phrase 'Son of the Blessed One' is equivalent to the phrase 'Son of God' and as Jesus implied in his speech in the temple on Psalm 110 it also indicated that the Messiah was more than a man for the psalm itself pointed towards his divine status.

Antiphon. The Lord says to my lord, 'Sit at my right hand until I make your enemies your footstool. … the Lord has sworn and will not change his mind, 'You are a priest for ever according to the order of Melchizedek.' (Psalm 110:1, 4).

Antiphon. As I watched in the night visions, I saw one like a human being (Aram *one like a son of man*) coming with the clouds of heaven. And he came to the Ancient One and was presented before him. To him was given dominion and glory and kingship, that all peoples, nations and languages should serve him. His dominion is an everlasting dominion that shall not pass away, and his kingship is one that shall never be destroyed. (Daniel 7:13–14).

'The high priest tore his clothes' and charged Jesus with blasphemy, and those in attendance 'condemned him as deserving of death'.

The supplementary messianic statements in Psalm 110 and Daniel 7:13–14 implied that he had divine status as 'Son of God' and also a human status as 'Son of Man'. His response included both his identity and prophecies about the future.

In symbolic form, the final response that Jesus conveyed to the readers of the Gospel of Mark came in two parts, one pertaining to the present and one pertaining to the future.

I am the Messiah (Human/Divine)
I am the Son of the Blessed One (Divine)

I am the Son of Man, coming with the clouds of heaven (Human)
I have an everlasting dominion (Divine)

This is the final message that Mark conveyed to his readers.

Jesus was taken to the Roman authorities and charged – not with the 'blasphemy' which was perceived as deserving death – but only with the political crime of being the Messiah, the prophesied 'King of the Jews' (Mark 15:2, 9, 12). In the end, the Romans crucified him for political reasons. 'The inscription of the charge against him' said simply, 'The King of the Jews' (Mark 15:26). Jesus had ended up dying as a political agitator but in the background this was caused by his 'blasphemy' during the trial.

In Mark's narrative, during the years of Jesus' public ministry, people who met him, who spoke to him, or who heard about him did not know his identity. It may be presumed that even before he was born, as a child, or a teen, or an adult until his baptism by John the Baptist – all episodes not discussed in Mark – then his identity had been a secret. This would allow Jesus to grow and mature into an adult in the Jewish community in a normal human fashion. The messianic secret likely extended throughout his life until his death (Mark 14:33–37). The lack of reliable written information about Jesus during his lifetime of about 35 years is accounted for by the messianic secret.

At the end of his life, Mark referred to a centurion who was facing the cross and witnessed his death, say, 'Truly this was God's Son! (Mark 15;39). For the Roman officer, this admission would not have a Christian content, but Mark clearly saw it as an acknowledgement that Jesus was more than a man.[15]

---

[15] Mark 15:39, fn. g. NJB.

The Protevangelium in the Gospel of Mark

The Old Testament does not contain any source for the three messianic statements by unclean spirits in Mark. The New Testament is also ruled out because during the public ministry of Jesus it had not yet been written. There is only one other outstanding document that belonged to neither, the Protevangelium, which discussed the birth of Jesus as well as his identity. It is an ancient work, with many copies in existence and a history that goes back almost 2000 years.

From his redaction-critical analysis of the Greek copies of the Protevangelium, Zervos (2019:203–204) argued that the document was not an 'expansion', elaboration', or 'development' of the canonical infancy narratives. Rather, *he proposed that it was an 'expansion', 'elaboration', and 'development of an early, non-canonical strata of material, some of which seem to have existed before the gospels of the New Testament, or possibly written concurrently with them.*

With this as a token, one may look for such a source which may have existed before the canonical infancy narratives in Matthew and Luke. The earliest canonical gospel is that of Mark and it has no infancy narratives. It is well known, however, that both Matthew and Luke have drawn upon Mark in the writing of their gospels. The Protevangelium is not explicitly noted during the public ministry of Jesus in Mark and could not have been written down until after the death of Jesus because of the messianic secret. The biblical sources confirm that Mary was the mother of Jesus, that she lived during the public ministry of Jesus, and that she continued to live in a Christian community after the death of Jesus.

> Antiphon. Meanwhile, standing near the cross of Jesus were his mother, and his mother's sister, Mary the wife of Clopas and Mary Magdalene. When Jesus saw his mother and the disciple whom he loved standing beside her, he said to his mother, 'Woman, here is your son.' Then he said to the disciple, 'Here is your mother'. And from that hour the disciple took her into his own home. (John 19:25–27).

After the ascension of Jesus on Mount Olivet, near Jerusalem, a sabbath day's journey away, the disciples of Jesus then returned to Jerusalem.

> Antiphon. When they entered the city, they went to the room upstairs where they were staying, Peter and John, and James, and Andrew, Philip and Thomas, Bartholomew and Matthew, James son of Alphaeus, and Simon the Zealot, and Judas son of James. All these were constantly devoting themselves to prayer, together with certain women, including Mary the mother of Jesus, as well as his brothers. (Acts 1:13–14).

Mary herself was obligated to be silent about the identity of Jesus until after his death. The Protevangelium, although in Mary's mind, would not exist outside of it throughout the period of the messianic secret. A suggested date for its first publication would be around 35–50 CE and it would be based on the testimony of Mary herself who had treasured its secrets for the protection of Jesus from his conception until his death. Like all the canonical material, this original version would have been written in Greek and it probably originated in Syria.

If copies had been written between 35–40 CE, it would not appear in the Gospel of Mark which deals with the public ministry between 30–33 CE. However, Mark who wrote his Gospel between 65–70 CE may have had access to it. Similarly, other early canonical sources such as the letters of Paul and Hebrews may have had access to it.

The Protevangelium is the source of the messianic information provided by the unclean spirits in the Gospel of Mark. Although no manuscript had been written, the facts that it conveyed were available in real time to unclean spirits who were there at the time. The Protevangelium would be a faithful record of the birth and related events since it is based on the testimony of Mary, soon after the death of Jesus. In this regard, the Syriac text is probably the most accurate copy of her testimony since it is the second oldest text available, and it appears to have been generated in the presumed area where the original version was created.

Before proceeding, it is necessary to establish a base point in the historiography of the Protevangelium since up until now it has wandered the world without a home and a date. A useful focus is the infancy narrative of Jesus, and one can assign the birth of Jesus in the Protevangelium to correspond to the birth of Jesus in the Gospel of Matthew. Most biblical scholars and ancient historians believe that the birth date of Jesus is around 4 to 6 BCE which is based on King Herod's reign in Matthew and the subtraction of the age of about 30 years from the beginning of the public ministry of Jesus. It is interesting for the modern scholar to know that the Protevangelium also associated the birth of Jesus with Herod's reign, and this provides an ideal point to link the sources. The date 5 BCE will be taken to mark the birth of Jesus in the Protevangelium and synchronize it with the canonical material. Other events in the Protevangelium are then easily traced because of the wealth of its internal controls.

It is also interesting that all the events in the Protevangelium take place in the age of the Old Testament, and none take place in the age of the New Testament. It sits on the borderline between the two. The Protevangelium is a prophetic text that links the two ages.

The Protevangelium speaks of more than the identity of Jesus, however, since it also describes the identity of Mary and her parents over a period of about 12 years from before the conception of Jesus. Mark could not reveal Jesus' identity within his Gospel until after the day of his death. However, the secret specifically applied to Jesus. Mark could exploit his narrative by providing messianic messages by unclean spirits that applied to Mary at a time before the conception of Jesus. The following text is such a message, publicly spoken to Mary by an angel at a time when Jesus had not yet been conceived.

> Antiphon. And the angel of the Lord said, "Not so, Mary; for the power of the Lord shall overshadow you; wherefore also the Holy One to be born of you shall be called the Son of the Most High. And you shall call his name Jesus; for he shall save his people from their sins." (Protevangelium 11.3, Closs, 2025).

The message of the angel revealed that 'Jesus', the future son of Mary, has the divine nature of the Holy One and also that he would be called 'the Son of the Most High'. Unclean spirits at that time would be aware of this message since before the angel appeared to Mary there had been a disturbance in Jerusalem.

Antiphon. And she [Mary] took the pitcher and went out to draw water, and behold, a voice said, "Hail, you who have received grace, the Lord is with you; blessed are you among women." And she looked around, to the right and to the left, to see where this voice came from. And, trembling, she returned to her house and put down the pitcher. And taking the purple, she sat down on her seat and drew it out. (Protevangelium 11.1, Closs, 2024).

The voice that Mary heard is the 'voice of heaven' – the 'Voice of God' – and is the same as the 'voice from heaven' that addressed Jesus at his baptism (Mark 1:11).

This voice was heard in Jerusalem at a time shortly before the annunciation to Mary. Mary herself, 'looked around, to the right and to the left, to see where the voice came from' and then 'trembling, she returned to her house'. Not only Mary, but others would hear the divine voice, including unclean spirits who would hasten to find Mary to hear and see what was going on.

With respect, to the title 'Son of the Most High', it has been seen earlier that it is equivalent to the title 'Son of God'. Both titles can be derived from the above annunciation text in the Protevangelium, and both can be applied to Jesus as messianic messages from unclean spirits.

The structure of the annunciation harmonizes with the words of Jesus at his trial in Mark's gospel where he identifies himself by referring to both his human status and his divine status. In reference to the 'son of Mary', Jesus reveals his human status as 'son of Man'. In reference to 'Son of the Most High' = 'Son of God', Jesus reveals his divine status. The account of the trial also shows the influence of the Protevangelium since some of his self-references pertain to his divine status and others to his human status.

Both Mark and the Protevangelium reveal that Jesus has both a human nature and a divine nature although he is but one person. In the future, theologians would describe this situation of having two natures in one person with a specialized terminology.[16] The Protevangelium and Mark exhibit the earliest period in the development of this concept.

The unclean spirit who referenced Jesus as the 'Holy One of God' used the divine title 'Holy One' favoured by Isaiah and links it to the divine title 'Son of the Most High', applied to 'Jesus' who is the son of Mary and also the Son of the Holy One.

Given that the three unclean spirits in Mark cite titles of Jesus from the Protevangelium indicates that Mark had access to it. This also validates Zervos' insights. If Mark had the Protevangelium when he prepared his account of the public ministry of Jesus then this work preceded all the canonical scriptures in the New Testament because all of these were written after the death of Jesus.

---

[16] Later theologians would refer to this as a 'hypostatic union', a technical term in Christian theology to describe the union of Christ's humanity and divinity in one person.

One of the shortcomings in the Gospel of Mark is that there is no reference to the idea that Jesus is a descendant of David. This may be an unintended omission in Mark because the Protevangelium provides evidence that his mother Mary is of the house of David.

> Antiphon. And there was a council of the priests, saying, "Let us make a veil for the temple of the Lord." And the high priest said, "Call to me the undefiled virgins of the tribe of David." And the officers went and sought and found seven virgins. And the high priest remembered the child Mary that she was of the tribe of David and undefiled before God. And the officers went and fetched her. (Protevangelium 12.1, Closs, 2024).

In this instance, the high priest deliberately mentions that Mary is a descendant of David. Jesus, the son of Mary, was raised as a Jew. The question of matrilineality is very complex in Judaism.[17] But, in this case, Jesus would be a Jew and a descendant of David.

Given the messianic secret in Mark, the three messianic messages by unclean spirits, the voice of God heralding Mary and the annunciation to her in the Protevangelium, the teaching of Jesus in the temple on Psalm 110, and the description in the trial of Jesus' and his response to the high priest, all indicate that Mark had access to the Protevangelium. It also indicates that Jesus is the son of Mary who is of the house of David.

It is important in analysing the Protevangelium that its internal nature be considered. This is initially shown by its very contents which expire at the time of Herod's massacre. Every incident in the Protevangelium takes place in the age of the Old Testament. The New Testament will feel the consequences of the Protevangelium, but it cannot be evaluated by working through the New Testament as previous commentators have done, including myself in the original version of this work.

In this edition, I will analyze the Protevangelium by emphasizing that it was written in the age of the Old Testament. Since it precedes the age of the New Testament it will eventually help us to understand some of the development of the canonical scriptures of the New Testament. One example of this has already been seen through the preceding arguments about the messianic secret in the Gospel of Mark and how it revealed that Mark had access to the Protevangelium.

In general, the Protevangelium lies on the border line between the ages of the Old Testament and the New Testament. It is a prophetic text – witnessed by Mary the mother of Jesus – that is associated with the age of the Old Testament, but it also looks ahead to the age of the New Testament. In the analysis of the Protevangelium and the commentary attached to it, only references from the Old Testament will be used. The very fact that it can be understood without any reference to the New Testament shows that it is a product of the age of the Old Testament.

One consequence of this work has already been demonstrated because scholars now have a better appreciation of the Gospel of Mark through its association with the Protevangelium.

---

[17] See, Wikipedia, 'Matrilineality in Judaism'.

The Protevangelium of James

Joachim's Offering

1.1 In the annals of the twelve tribes of Israel, few men were as rich as Joachim. He always brought a double portion of offerings to the Lord, saying, "What I bring in excess shall be for the whole people and the other shall be a sin offering for the Lord, as a propitiation for me."

1.2 Now the great day of the Lord was at hand and the children of Israel were bringing their offerings. But, on this occasion, Reuben stood up and said, "It is not lawful for you to be first among those who bring offerings to the Lord because you have begotten no offspring for Israel."

1.3 At this, Joachim became greatly distressed. He went to the records of the twelve tribes of the people, saying, "I will look for myself to determine whether I am the only one who has not produced offspring for Israel." His searches were fruitless – all the righteous had indeed raised up offspring for Israel. And then he remembered that God had granted the patriarch Abraham, in his old age, a son, Isaac.

1.4 And so, Joachim, deeply grieved, did not return to his wife but went into the wilderness. There he pitched his tent – fasting for forty days and forty nights. In his own mind he said, "I shall refuse food and drink until the Lord my God visits me. My prayers shall be food and drink to me."

Commentary

1.1.a. Joachim may be compared to his namesake 'Joachim' in Daniel 13:1 who is attested in the public record in Israel.[18] This person was rich and regarded with great honour. In this he was like Mary's father. This comparison is interesting because 'Anna', Mary's mother, also had great similarities to the wife of Joachim's namesake. She was a person 'who feared the Lord' and whose parents were righteous, and she had been trained according to the law of Moses' (Daniel 13.2–3). And this was the case with Anna as will be seen in the early chapters of the Protevangelium.

Not only was Joachim rich and honourable, but he was also very generous. He would always bring a double offering to the temple, half for himself to offer to God as a sin-offering and the other half for the people. In the Greek, his generosity is expressed through an imperfect tense indicating that it was habitual (Amann,

---

[18] This has also been noted by Hock, 1995:33, fn. 1:1.

1910:181). Joachim also reminded people of Tobit, who 'walked 'in the ways of truth and righteousness' all the days of his life' (Tobit 1:3). The comparison is a good one because of his generosity.

> Antiphon. But I alone went off to Jerusalem for the festivals, as is prescribed for all Israelites by an everlasting decree. I would hurry off to Jerusalem with the first fruits of the crops and the firstlings of the flock, the tithes of the cattle, and the first shearings of the sheep. I would give these to the priests, the sons of Aaron, at the altar; likewise the tenth of the grain, wine, olive oil, pomegranates, figs, and the rest of fruits to the sons of Levi who ministered at Jerusalem. Also, for six years I would save up a second tenth in money and go and distribute it in Jerusalem. (Tobit 1:6–7).

The wealth of Joachim is derived from him being a master of flocks (4.3).

1.2.a. Joachim brought his offerings to the temple on 'the great day of the Lord'. This was likely the 'sabbath'. It is described in the Priestly version of the creation story as something that is divinely instituted. 'God blessed the seventh day and made it holy, because on that day he *rested* after all his work in creating'. (Genesis 2:3, NJB).[19]

As Joachim brought his offerings to the temple, he was confronted by Reuben who was angry that Joachim is the 'first' among those who bring offerings to the Lord'. Joachim is rich and generous and brings offerings not only for himself but in equal measure for the people. This would create a logistics problem. Not only his offering but also the equal offering for the people had to be gathered and distributed. Because of his habitual generosity it would be preferable that he be 'first' in line. It would also make him well known among the priests in the temple.

Amann, 1910:183, noted that Greek commentators see Reuben as a namesake of the tribe of Reuben. His appearance here is symbolic: Reuben represents the opposition of the tribe of Reuben, which had the birthright (Genesis 35:23–26) and the tribe of Judah, from which comes the Messiah.[20]

In Israelite history, Reuben, the firstborn son of Jacob 'went and lay with Bilhah', the concubine of his father (Genesis 35:22). Upon his deathbed, Jacob removed the birthright (as firstborn) from Reuben because of this afront (Genesis 49:4). A comment in 1 Chronicles 5:1–2 makes the same point and argues that the birthright was transferred to the sons of Joseph. David is descended from Joseph and one of the descendants of David was prophesied to be the Messiah. Classical rabbinical sources argue that the birthright had included the right to become ruler over the tribes and the priests, a right transferred to the tribe of Judah and the Levites. This problem may also be the source of Reuben's grievance.

In any case, Reuben confronts Joachim and says that 'it is not lawful for you to be first among those who bring offerings to the Lord because you have begotten no children for Israel'. This accusation is functional in the narrative development. However, the charge itself is artificial since the problem of not having children

---

[19] Genesis 3, fn. a. NJB. The Sabbath (*shabbat*) is of divine institution: on that day God himself rested (*shabat*). The word *shabbat*, however, is avoided here since according to the Priestly author, the Sabbath was not imposed until the giving of the law on Sinai, when it then became the sign of the covenant, Exodus 31:12–17. Even at the creation, however, God set an example which must be followed (Exodus 20:11; 31:17).
[20] Wikipedia, 'Reuben (son of Jacob)'.

is accepted as a natural phenomenon in sacred scripture. Such an accusation has been examined and found wanting.

There are only a few cases when childlessness is imposed as a result of evildoing. In Leviticus 20:20–21, it is punishment for egregious cases of sexual misconduct. In 2 Samuel 6:23 it is because Michal mocked David for honouring the Lord by leaping and dancing in front of the ark of the covenant and despised him in her heart (2 Samuel 6:16) and insulted him as a vulgar fellow for shamelessly uncovering himself before the eyes of the servants and maids (2 Samuel 6:20). In Genesis 20:17–18, in Abimelech's court, infertility is used rhetorically to demonstrate the Lord's response to his action in taking Sarah.[21]

In the case of Joachim's wife, however, her lack of fertility is simply regarded as "natural". Her situation is similar to that of the five biblical women said to be barren – Sarah (Genesis 11:30), Rebekah (Genesis 25:21), Rachel (Genesis 29:31), Samson's mother (Judges 13:2–3), and Hannah (1 Samuel 1:5).

They are all introduced as barren before we know little else about them. What little we do know, in the cases of Rebekah and Rachel, is entirely positive. Neither the text, nor any exegetical reason assumes that they are barren because they have been punished for any wrongdoing (Baden, 2011:18).

Baden, 2011:21, shows that with respect to these five women, there are a number of commonalities that extend across the specific narratives.

1. They are introduced as barren; their infertility is, for the most part, their defining characteristic.
2. There is divine intervention: the Lord grants each woman fertility – again without any indication that the woman did anything new to deserve this blessing.
3. Each woman gives birth to a major figure in Israel's mythic past: Isaac, Jacob (and Esau), Joseph (and Benjamin), Samson, and Samuel.

In all of these cases barrenness is an obstacle that serves to highlight God's power over history. Barrenness is regarded as "natural" and is clearly not a curse. It is simply an obstacle and God's power will overcome it. When this rhetorical use of barrenness is recognized, it forces an adjustment in how we evaluate the perception of infertility in ancient Israel. It is not clear from the biblical texts that barrenness is a particular concern in its own right; it is either the logical mechanism by which Yahweh's promise of progeny is challenged or a single element among others about God's power to alter the normal course of human life. The societal standing or treatment of the barren woman is not at issue in any of these texts (Baden, 2011: 23).

1.3.a.   In the honour-shame society in which Joachim lived, however, the challenge to his social place caused great distress. It placed him in an awkward position since he had no children to prove that God had indeed blessed him. Overwhelmed by confusion, he wondered if he was really the only one among all the just without posterity. He went to the records of the twelve tribes of the people. He searched to see if he was the only one who had not raised up offspring for Israel.

---

[21] Joel S. Baden, "The Nature of Barrenness in the Hebrew Bible," in *Disability Studies and Biblical Literature* (Palgrave Macmillan, 2011, 22.)

A glimmer of hope, however, entered Joachim's mind when he remembered that Abraham had a son, 'Isaac', in his extreme old age. Is it possible, he argued, that God might have mercy on him as well? (Amann, 1910:183).

> Antiphon. The Lord dealt with Sarah as he had said, and the Lord did for Sarah as he had promised. Sarah conceived and bore Abraham a son in his old age, at the time of which God had spoken to him. (Genesis 21:1–2).

1.4.a.   This partially explains Joachim's resolve to withdraw into the country. In doing so, he not only wants to avoid his wife – thereby increasing his penance – but also primarily to implore the Lord and receive a sign that his prayer will be answered. (Amann, 1910:183–184).

His wife Anna would hear of the altercation because it was a public event. She would understand the loneliness they both felt at not having children. She would also know from Joachim's workmen that he had retired to the country to fast and to pray.

As will become apparent in (4.3), the wilderness is not an arid region but a grassy area suitable for grazing flocks. That section also leads us to understand that Joachim pitched his tent not far from where his flocks were grazing.

Joachim will fast for forty days and forty nights as once did Moses and Elijah. Is it an absolute fast?

The author's expression and a comparison with the texts indicate that it was (Amann, 1910:184–185).

> Antiphon. He [Moses] was there with the Lord for forty days and forty nights; he neither ate bread nor drank water. And he wrote on the tablets the words of the covenant, the ten commandments. (Exodus 34:28).

> Antiphon. He [Elijah] got up, and ate and drank; then he went in the strength of that food for forty days and forty nights to Horeb the mount of God. (1 Kings 19:8).

In his solitude Joachim hoped to have a visit from the Lord, that is to say, a message announcing that his prayer will be answered (Amann, 1910:185).

The prayer of Joachim will be food and drink for him.

> Antiphon. Your words were found, and I ate them, and your words became to me a joy and the delight of my heart; for I am called by your name, O Lord, God of hosts. (Jeremiah 15:16).

Anna's Lament

2.1   Anna, his wife, sang two dirges; twice did she lament.

"I will mourn my widowhood;
I will mourn my childlessness."

2.2   Now the great day of the Lord was at hand and Judith her handmaid said, "How long do you intend to humble your soul? Behold, the day of the Lord is nigh and it is not lawful for you to mourn. Here, take this headband. The mistress of work gave it to me, but it is not proper that I should wear it. It has a royal appearance, and I am but a handmaid."

2.3   But Anna said, "Get away from me! I shall never do it. The Lord has greatly humbled me. Who knows? Perhaps a wicked person has given it to you and now you have come to make me share in your sin!" Then Judith said, "What evil could I wish upon you since the Lord has shut up your womb so as to give you no fruit for Israel."

2.4   And Anna was very sad. She then took off her mourning garments, washed her head, and put on her wedding garments. About the ninth hour she went down to her garden to walk and seeing a laurel tree, she sat in its shade. And she pleaded with the Lord, saying, "O God of our fathers, bless me and hear my prayer. Just as you blessed the womb of Sarah and gave her a son Isaac."

Commentary

2.1.a.   Anna's story opens with a twofold lament employing graceful poetry. The introduction to Anna is more restrained than that for Joachim. Without telling us anything about Anna's past, it shows her grief, revealing small details of her domestic life (Amann, 1910:185). She bewails her widowhood – her perception of her loneliness – because Joachim had left for the country. Like Joachim, she bewails her childlessness.

2.1.b.   It is well-known that Anna also has a namesake, 'Hannah', in 1 Samuel 1. Hannah is the mother of the prophet Samuel, and the concept is reinforced because parts of Anna's story are akin to those of Hannah. In the present moment, like the mother of Samuel, Anna expresses her innermost feelings in verse, providing an insight into the complaint that escapes from her lips (Amann, 1910:185).

Several words appear to be Hebrew expressions, but this does not presume a Hebrew original. The author may have borrowed them from the Greek of the Septuagint. Moreover, similar turnings of phrase are not unknown in classical Greek (Amann, 1910:185).

2.2.a. The *great day of the Lord,* as before, marks the sabbath. As is customary, the sabbath is often celebrated at home as is the case here. The narrative assumes an interval between the sabbath at which Joachim was insulted and the present sabbath for, as Amann indicated, Anna is already bemoaning her 'widowhood'.

A. Meyer suggested that this episode draws on the story of the heroine Judith of Bethulia in the Book of Judith.[22] The transposition to the Protevangelium is transparent. Anna is characterized as the heroine while her handmaid takes the name of 'Judith'. The narrative from 2.2–2.4 is shaped by that story.

> Antiphon. When Judith had stopped crying out to the God of Israel, and had ended all these words, she rose from where she lay prostrate. She called her maid and went down into the house where she lived on sabbaths and on her festal days. She removed the sackcloth she had been wearing, took off her widow's garments, bathed her body with water, and anointed herself with precious ointment. She combed her hair, put on a tiara, and dressed herself in the festive attire that she used to wear while her husband Manasseh was living. (Judith 10:1–3).

It should be noted that 'the great day of the Lord' in the Protevangelium is identified with 'the sabbath' in Judith and this provides independent affirmation of that association. One also notes that Judith is a widow, and that Anna is characterized in the same way (although, inappropriately).

The expression *to humble your soul* is taken from the Septuagint. It indicates not only the inner humility imposed on the Day of Atonement but also exterior mortification, especially fasting (Amann, 1910:185–186).

> Antiphon. This rest shall be Sabbata of sabbaths to you, and you shall humble your souls; it is a perpetual precept. (Leviticus 16:31, NETS).

However, with the sabbath at hand, it was time to get ready.

> Antiphon. This is the day that the Lord has made; let us rejoice and be glad in it. (Psalm 118:24).

> Antiphon. She fasted all the days of her widowhood, except the day before the sabbath and the sabbath itself, the day before the new moon and the day of the new moon, and the festivals and days of rejoicing of the house of Israel. (Judith 8:5).

2.2.b. It is for this reason that the handmaid pointed out to her mistress that it was time to stop mourning. At the same time, she offered to dress her in festive clothing and to encircle her head with a precious ornament, an ornate headband, that served to retain the hair and when attached to the bottom of a Persian tiara, becomes a royal ornament (Amann, 1910:186).

---

[22] A. Meyer. Commentary in Hennecke, *Neutestamentliche Apokryphen in deutscher Uebersetzung und mit Einleitungen,* Tubingue and Leipzig, 1904.

The offering of the ornament to Anna supports her dignity. Only Anna could have worn the headband because it was suitable for the daughter of kings. Similarly, the problem with Reuben insulting and ordering Joachim to the back of the line (1.2) may be related to Anna if she is of the house of David. These byproducts in the narrative may indicate that Mary's mother is of the house of David. Regardless of the specific arguments, there is stricter evidence in (10.1) in which the high priest specifically identifies Mary as being of the house of David.

How did the handmaid get hold of the ornament? The text is ambiguous as is the reference to the 'mistress of work'. By reference to the Syriac version, Amann argues that the 'mistress of work' is one who employed the handmaid previously in another household. Using the Syriac version in this way, it is important to recognize that it is the second oldest copy of the Protevangelium in existence and that it also hails from the area in which the Protevangelium may have originally been written.

2.3.a. Anna indignantly rejects the headband that was offered to her by her handmaid. The Greek aorist in the sentence suggests that it is the misery of Anna that causes such an outburst (Amann, 1910:187). She justifies her fears by saying that perhaps a wicked person had given her the headband and she has now come to involve herself in the duplicity. Outraged by this suspicion, the handmaid vents her anger against her mistress. She would not willingly wish evil upon her since it would be pointless as Anna is already afflicted with the greatest of misfortunes, childlessness. The insult addressed to Anna is like the harsh words that Reuben had said to Joachim. The couple has now suffered the same criticism, a consequence of the mean-spirited actions by others. Nevertheless, their childlessness is a natural phenomenon and is not punishment for any evil that they have done. It will be up to the Lord to justify them.

2.3.b. The story of Anna with respect to the headband and the handmaid is inspired by the episode in Tobit 2:11–14. There is more than one way to understand this incident in the Greek text, but Amann has translated it by considering the Syriac version (Amann, 1910:187). The story is a skilful blending of Tobit 2:11–14 and Judith 10:1–3).

> Antiphon. At that time, also, my wife, Anna earned money at women's work. She used to send what she made to the owners and they would pay wages to her. One day, the seventh of Dystrus, when she cut off a piece she had woven and sent it to the owners, they paid her full wages and also gave her a kid for a meal. When she returned to me, the kid began to bleat. So I called her and said, "Where did you get this kid? It is surely not stolen is it? Return it to the owners; for we have no right to eat anything stolen." But she said to me, "It was given to me as a gift in addition to my wages." But I did not believe her, and told her to return it to the owners. I became flushed with anger against her over this. Then she replied to me, "Where are your acts of charity? Where are your righteous deeds? These things are known about you!" (Tobit 2:11–14).

In the Protevangelium, the author has substituted Anna for Tobit and the handmaid for Tobit's wife. The offer of the kid is replaced by that of the headband (inspired by the Judith episode). The narrative action of the plot is akin to that of the Tobit and Judith stories.

Of special significance here is that Tobit's wife is also named Anna. Both Anna, the wife of Tobit, and Hannah, the mother of Samuel, are namesakes of our protagonist. Thus, the incident in the Protevangelium is a like-in-kind to that related in Tobit with suitable transpositions. The author has used the scriptures to find biblical portrayals of those named "Anna," suggesting that this is truly the name of Mary's mother.

2.4.a.   Anna is grieved over her own behaviour. She recognizes the validity of the observations of her handmaid, abandons her mourning clothes and dresses in her finest apparel, the attire that she wore on her wedding day.

About the ninth hour of the day – the middle of the afternoon – Anna descended into the garden to walk. The solemnity of the day prohibited any work, and this is the sole recreation that she could give to herself. She sees a laurel tree and sits in its shade. It is there that she pleads to the Lord – who being all powerful – can assist her. She then thought of Sarah, who God had blessed in her old age, and she had received a son. She prayed that she too might have such a blessing.

2.4.b.   The events, so far considered, of Joachim and Anna may seem implausible as history but can be understood as the rewriting of Old Testament scenes in order to apply them anew to fit Joachim and Anna. The description of Mary's parents is taken, at times almost verbatim, from the stories of Hannah, Anna and Tobit, Judith, and more distantly Abraham and Sarah. They are written to make Mary's origins intelligible against the background of Old Testament expectations. Mary and later her son Jesus are to be seen as embedded within the fulfillment of the prophetic word in ancient Israel.

The texts make no attempt to interpret the full or contextual meaning of the Old Testament but focus on a particular prophetic future underlying The Book of Mary and a prophetic future for Israel.

Anna's Song

3.1   Turning her eyes towards the heavens, Anna saw a nest of sparrows in the laurel tree. And she sang a dirge deep within herself:

> Woe is me! Who begot me?
> What womb brought me forth?
> I am a curse in your presence,
> a curse before the people of Israel.
> I am reproached and I am mocked,
> thrust out of the temple of the Lord.

3.2   Woe is me! To whom shall I be compared?
> Not to the birds of the heavens,
> for even the birds of the heavens
> are fruitful before You, O Lord.
>
> Woe is me! To whom shall I be compared?
> Not to the beasts of the earth,
> for even the beasts of the earth
> are fruitful before You, O Lord.
>
> Woe is me! To whom shall I be compared?
> Not to the waters [round about],
> for even the waters [round about]
> are fruitful before You, O Lord.

3.3   Woe is me! To whom shall I be compared?
> Not to the earth in due season,
> for even the earth is fruitful
> and praises You, O Lord."

Commentary

3.1.a.   The sight of a nest of sparrows is enough to make Anna's grievances rush out. The spectacle of this happy fertility given by God to creatures that seem so puny reminds Joachim's wife of her sad situation.

The lament that escapes Anna's lips is simple, but its monotony is not without charm. There are five stanzas. In the first, Anna curses the day of her birth. This includes a reference to a contempt received in the temple of the Lord, but this may just be the hurt that had been done to Joachim coming back to haunt her (Amann:1910:190–191).

> Antiphon. After this Job opened his mouth and cursed the day of his birth. Job said: "Let the day perish in which I was born, and the night that said, 'A man-child is conceived.' Let that day be darkness! May God above not seek it, or light shine on it." (Job 3:1–4).

3.2.b. Rather than recalling the plaint of Job, the scene pertaining to Anna is more directly related to Tobit. For Tobit, the sparrows marked the sealing of his eyes; for Anna, the sparrows recalled the sealing of her womb. Like Tobit she rues her fate and is stirred to sing a song of woe.

> Tobit: Washed himself and went into his courtyard (Tobit 2:9)
> Anna: Washed her head and went to the garden to walk (2.4)

> Tobit: Slept by the wall of the courtyard (Tobit 2:9)
> Anna: Seeing a laurel tree, she sat in its shade (2.4)

> Tobit: Did not know that there were sparrows on the wall (Tobit 2:10)
> Anna: Saw a nest of sparrows in the laurel tree (3.1)

> Tobit: Wept, and with groaning began to pray (Tobit 3:1)
> Sarah: Was grieved in spirit and wept (Tobit 3:10); with hands outstretched towards the window, she prayed (Tobit 3:11)
> Anna: Sang a dirge deep within herself (3.1)

> Sarah: I turn my face to you, and raise my eyes towards you (Tobit 3:12)
> Anna: Turning her eyes towards the heavens (3.1)

> Tobit: It is better for me to die than to see so much distress in my life and to listen to insults (Tobit 3:6)
> Sarah: Command that I be released from the earth and not listen to such reproaches any more (Tobit 3:13)
> Anna: I am a curse in your presence … I am reproached and I am mocked (3.1)

Given the similarities and the author's previous interest in Tobit, it is reasonable to think that the setting of the stage for Anna's song of woe is inspired by sundry elements in Tobit.

3.2.c–3.3. In the next four stanzas, all constructed on the same model, Anna looks to nature to find arguments against the Lord because of a fruitfulness that she has been denied. The parallelism in the last four stanzas is strictly maintained. The birds of the sky and the beasts of the field (cf. Genesis 1), the waters and the earth, are all in turn cited as examples of fertility (Amann, 1910:190–191).

Hock, 1995:37, fn. 3:4–8, includes an extra stanza since there is a doubling of the "beasts of the earth" stanza into separate stanzas for "domestic animals" and for "animals in the wild." He notes that the manuscripts differ in the number of stanzas, the order of stanzas, and the wording. In terms of the antiquity of manuscripts, Hock is translating the earliest Greek manuscript, but the second oldest of all is the Syriac. Since it has fewer stanzas it may preserve an older form than what is found in the oldest Greek manuscript.

The Protevangelium of James, Chapter 4

The Annunciation (Anna)

4.1   And behold an angel of the Lord appeared to her and said, "Anna, Anna, the Lord has heard your prayer. You shall conceive and bring forth a child and your offspring shall be known throughout the world." And Anna said, "As the Lord my God lives, if I bear a child, whether male or female, I will offer it to the Lord my God, and it shall serve him all the days of its life."

4.2   And behold, two messengers came and said to her, "Behold, Joachim your husband, is coming with his flocks. An angel of the Lord was sent to him saying, 'Joachim, Joachim, the Lord God has heard your prayer. Go down from here; behold, your wife Anna shall conceive.'"

4.3   And Joachim went down and called his herdsmen. He said, "Bring me ten female lambs without spot or blemish; they shall be for the Lord my God. And bring me twelve tender calves; they shall be for the priests and the elders. And also bring a hundred goats for all the people."

4.4   And behold, Joachim came with his flocks and Anna, who stood at the gate, saw him coming. She immediately ran to him, throwing her arms around his neck, exclaiming, "Now I know that the Lord my God has greatly blessed me. For behold, the widow is no longer a widow and I who was childless shall conceive." And Joachim rested the first day in his house.

Commentary

4.1.a.   Without any transition, Anna's prayer has been answered. The annunciation to Anna is similar to other announcements of divine intervention with respect to female figures in the Old Testament who were childless. In this case it is also closely related to the annunciation of births of two classical nazirites, Samson and Samuel.

The root meaning of nazirite (Hebrew *názir*) is connected with 'vow' in biblical Hebrew. Baruch Levine notes that literally the term *názir* means "one restricted, set apart." As defined in Numbers 6, a *názir* is "a person who had pledged under terms of a vow (*neder*) to restrict his behavior in several areas so as to attain a greater measure of holiness in his life."[23]

Thus, formally, Anna has made a nazirite vow on behalf of her future child to 'offer it to the Lord' and set it apart to serve the Lord all the days of its life.

---

[23] Baruch A. Levine, *Numbers 1–20: A New Translation with Introduction and Commentary* (New York: Doubleday, 1980:2215, 219.

The phenomenon of naziritism is a very ancient institution and one that persisted long after the biblical period. In the laws regarding naziritism in Numbers 6 there are both positive and negative nuances. Negative aspects pertain to the notions of restriction, abstinence, and self-denial and positive aspects to devotion, commitments and pledge.

> Antiphon. The Lord spoke to Moses, saying: Speak to the Israelites and say to them: When either men or women make a special vow, the vow of a nazirite, to separate themselves to the Lord, they shall separate themselves from wine and strong drink; they shall drink no wine vinegar or other vinegar, and shall not drink any grape juice or eat grapes, fresh or dried. All their days as nazirites they shall eat nothing that is produced by the grape-vine, not even the seeds or the skins. All the days of their nazirite vow no razor shall come upon the head; until the time is completed for which they separate themselves to the Lord, they shall be holy; they shall let the locks of the head grow long. All the days that they separate themselves to the Lord they shall not go near a corpse. Even if their father or mother, brother or sister, should die, they may not defile themselves; because their consecration to God is upon the head. All their days as nazirites they are holy to the Lord. (Numbers 6:1–8).

The fact that the sex of Anna's child is unknown does not preclude such a vow, since the legal code provides that 'either men or women' could 'make a special vow' and 'separate themselves to the Lord'. A central feature of this legislation is the emphasis on holiness: 'All their days as nazirites they are holy to the Lord'.

One of the restrictions imposed on nazirites is that 'they shall not go near a corpse'. Levine notes that the degree of restriction is more severe in the case of the nazirite than it is even with respect to ordinary priests. He compares the restrictions imposed on the nazirite to be as severe as those applicable to the high priest and infers that a high degree of purity was basic to the concept of naziritism (Levine, 1980:221).

4.1.b. It is interesting to compare Anna's vow with those of her two closest biblical models.

> Antiphon. There was a certain man of Zorah, of the tribe of the Danites, whose name was Manoah. His wife was barren, having borne no children. And the angel of the Lord appeared to the woman and said to her, 'Although you are barren, having borne no children, you shall conceive and bear a son. Now be careful not to drink wine or strong drink, or to eat anything unclean, for you shall conceive and bear a son. No razor is to come on his head, for the boy shall be a nazirite to God from birth. It is he who shall begin to deliver Israel from the hand of the Philistines.' (Judges 13:2–5).

In time, her son was born and was named Samson. Surprisingly, in his case, it is an angel of the Lord who placed the vow. The sex of her child is prespecified as a boy. Initially, the mother is to carry out some of the regulations imposed on nazirites because her son is a nazirite from birth. No indication is given about the strict restriction of nazirites to 'not go near a corpse'. Scholars understand that Samson is relieved of this restriction because he was a 'warrior nazirite' who would 'begin to deliver Israel from the hand of the Philistines'.

It appears that Anna follows the path of Samson most closely because they are both permanent nazirites in an ultimate sense because for Samson it is 'from birth' and for Anna's child it is 'all the days of its life'. It is likely that her child must carry out the same restrictions given to Samson. In the case of Anna, she carried out the restrictions imposed on Samson's mother when her child was very young as is demonstrated in (6.1). Since Samson avoided the restriction about not going near a corpse, then Anna's child was probably given the same leeway. At this time, nobody knew whether Anna's child would be a boy or a girl and what it meant when Anna proclaimed that her child would be a 'servant of the Lord'.

The story of Samuel begins with Elkanah who had two wives Hannah and Peninnah. Peninnah had children but Hannah had none. Every year they would go up to the house of the Lord at Shiloh to worship and to sacrifice. Peninnah would provoke Hannah severely to irritate her because the Lord had closed her womb. At Shiloh, after they had eaten and drunk, Hannah rose and presented herself before the Lord. She was deeply distressed and prayed to the Lord, and wept bitterly.

> Antiphon. She made this vow: 'O Lord of hosts, if only you will look on the misery of your servant, and remember me, and not forget your servant, but will give to your servant a male child, then I will set him before you as a nazirite until the day of his death. He shall drink neither wine nor intoxicants, and no razor shall touch his head.' (1 Samuel 1:10–11).

In this instance, Hannah makes a vow to bring up a male child who will be dedicated as a nazirite until the day of his death. She also agrees to follow some of the nazirite regulations, the same ones that were imposed on Samson. This further suggests that the same restrictions would have been placed on the child of Anna.

Eli the priest was sitting by the doorpost and heard her but thought she was drunk. After a brief discussion with Hannah about what was going on, Eli answered, 'Go in peace; the God of Israel grant the petition you have made of him.' And she said, 'Let your servant find favour in your sight.' (1 Samuel 1:17–18). Hannah left in peace. Then early in the morning they worshipped before the Lord and returned home. Elkanah and his wife Hannah resumed sexual activity and in due time she conceived and bore a son and named him Samuel.

Hannah decided, 'As soon as the child is weaned, I will bring him, that he may appear in the presence of the Lord, and remain there forever; I will offer him as a nazirite for all time' (1 Samuel 1:22).

In this instance, Samuel would become a nazirite when he was brought to the temple at Shiloh when he was about 3 years old. Samson would become a nazirite at his birth, and Mary's child would be a nazirite 'all the days of its life'.

It may be noticed that the term 'nazirite' appears in the stories of Samson and Samuel, but it does not appear in the case of Anna. Nevertheless, as noted above in (4.1.a), Levine observes that the term 'nazirite' is connected with 'vow' and it is the 'vow' that is most significant. Moreover, the Septuagint also depicts Samson and Samuel as nazirites in which the term 'nazirite' is ignored.

Re Samson:

> Antiphon. And he said to me, 'See, you are pregnant and shall bear a son. And now drink no wine or strong drink, and eat no unclean thing, for the boy shall be holy to God from the womb to the day of his death.' " (Judges B, 13:7, NETS).

Re Samuel:

> Antiphon. And she [Hannah] was deeply distressed in soul and prayed to the Lord, and weeping she wept and vowed a vow to the Lord saying "Adonai, Lord, Eloai, Sabaoth, if looking you will look on the humiliation of your slave and remember me and give me to your slave an offspring of men, and I will give him as one devoted before you until the day of his death, and wine and strong drink he shall not drink, and no iron shall come upon his head. (1 Reigns, 1:10–11, NETS).

This indicates that for Anna's child her vow is sufficient to indicate that it is 'dedicated' to God or 'holy to God'. This is evident in Anna's vow since her child is offered ('dedicated') to God and that it shall serve God all the days of its life.

In the case of nazirites with permanent vows, there appears to be a custom of not discussing it. With respect to Samson, the vow is revealed in its making. When Samson reveals his "secret" in a later confession, it will lead to his death (Judges 16:17–19. Similarly, in the case of Samuel, it is mentioned in Hannah's vow before he was conceived and then again at the beginning of his life as a prophet when he is given to the temple. No further mention of it is made in the story of Samuel. The same pattern applies to Anna, for it is in the vow that Anna had made, and the only other reference is spoken by Mary herself, who professed it when the angel asked her to be the mother of Jesus. She agreed and affirmed that she was 'the servant of the Lord – in his presence' (11.3).

With respect to Hannah, after she brought Samuel to the temple at Shiloh, she made a prayer to the Lord. She would then continue to return to Shiloh each year to offer the yearly sacrifice. Eli would then bless Elkanah and Hannah for the gift of Samuel to the Lord and said: 'May the Lord repay you with children by this woman for the gift that she made to the Lord'. And 'the Lord took note of Hannah; she conceived and bore three sons and two daughters'. (1 Samuel 2:19–21).

4.1.c. It is of interest to know of other female nazirites, of whom Queen Helena of Abiadene is probably the most famous. She died c. 50–56 CE with an account of her life given by Josephus, *Antiquities of the Jews*, Book 20, chs. 2, 4.3, and 5.2. She brought relief to the population of Jerusalem during the famine of 48 CE.

> Antiphon. It is related that Queen Helena, when her son went to war, said: "If my son returns in peace from the war, I shall be a nazirite for seven years. Her son returned from the war, and she observed a naziriteship for seven years. At the end of the seven years, she went up to the land [of Israel] and Beth Hillel ruled that she must be a nazirite for a further seven years. Towards the end of this seven years, she contracted ritual defilement, and so altogether she was a nazirite for twenty-one years. R. Judah said: she was only a nazirite for fourteen years. (Mishnah Nazir 19b).

Helena is an interesting example of a female nazirite for it shows that even a woman with children can become a nazirite. The intent of her vow is simply to set herself apart for the Lord to protect her child who had gone to war.

4.2.a. This section begins with the word 'behold' suggesting that Anna has just ended her prayer, and she received the information that will allow for the realization of the divine promise. Messengers have come to announce to her that her husband is readying himself to return. Amann (1910:193) observes that these two messengers are not angels, as some have thought, who are bringing the news. He says, prudently, that there is no reason to translate "messengers" as "angels" since the event that they have come to announce is entirely in the human order.

The messengers relate the story of the angelic annunciation to Joachim. The fact that Joachim too has received 'angelic news of the impending conception of their child – 'Anna shall conceive' – confirms that Anna was not dreaming.

4.2.b. On the other hand, citing different manuscript traditions, Hock, 1995:39, fn. 4:4, suggests that Joachim is told that 'Anna *is pregnant*' (perfect tense) or that 'Anna *will be pregnant*' (future tense) and that scholars differ among themselves over which reading to accept as original. He then asserts that 'those who decide on the future tense base their decision on a sexual connotation to the word rested in 4.4 citing Smid, 1965, *Commentary*, 41). And he entangles his argument by citing 'it is probable that the author understands 'Mary to have been the product of a miraculous conception', citing de Strycker, 1961, 81, n.3). Both of these arguments have little value.

In the annunciation to Anna in 4.1, the angel tells Anna that 'you shall conceive'. Hock, 1995:37, in his translation records the same message, 'you will conceive. This is in the future tense. Section, 4.2, begins with the word 'behold' implying that the messengers came suddenly after Anna had received her angelic visitation. Then the messengers begin their report with 'behold', indicating that suddenly Joachim would be coming. The messengers are ahead of Joachim, but he is on his way. They say that Joachim had received an angelic visitation that 'Anna shall conceive'. This is the same message that Anna had received, 'you shall conceive'. To say, 'Anna is pregnant' makes no sense since Joachim had not yet arrived. The narrative forbids it. After Joachim had received the news he had been hoping for, he was eager to get back, but he had to arrange an offering (4.3) for the temple. This would not happen instantly. Once this was done, he headed for home. The messengers, as expected, arrived before he did. Amann, 1910:193, makes these observations and also notes there is nothing in the text to presume a 'miraculous conception' since all the circumstances in the narrative create the opposite impression. Hock's objection makes little sense. One should not argue about the tenses of the verb when only one of them is consistent with the narrative.

4.3.a. Trusting in the angelic promise, Joachim is eager to be reunited with his wife. At the same time, he wants to give the Lord proof of his gratitude by preparing a large sacrifice He brings 'ten female lambs without spot or blemish' for the Lord, 'twelve tender calves' for the priests and the elders, and 'one hundred goats' for all the people. It is a large offering and the numbers indicate the logistics problem in bringing it to the temple. This is a sufficicient reason that the priests would want to deal with Joachim 'first' in (1.2) because he was habitual in bringing large offerings.

4.3.b. As first noted in (1.4), the wilderness into which Joachim retreated is not far from where he had many flocks and herdsmen working for him.

4.4.a. Suddenly, Joachim appears at the gate with a real herd that he had taken away from his flocks. Some manuscripts have added "with his shepherds" but Amann argues that these are not from the most authoritative copies. One may assume, however, that Joachim who was rich and highly esteemed, was not himself driving the flocks himself but had shepherds with him. The messengers that Joachim had sent on ahead of him would warn of his arrival. And Anna, who 'stood at the gate' saw him coming.

The Protevangelium suggests but does not say specifically that Anna and Joachim's house was in Jerusalem. However, this can be inferred from the direction of the narrative in subsequent chapters.

Regardless of where the house was located, the scene of the meeting of Anna and Joachim is one of the most gracious in all of the apocryphal literature. Popular piety liked to contemplate this encounter. It saw in the chaste embrace of the spouses, the prelude to the conception of Mary. For a long time, there was no other interpretation of this mystery than the touching scene in the Protevangelium. With great delicacy it is suggested that Mary's conception took place according to the natural order.

Immediately, upon seeing him, Anna rushes to Joachim and throws her arms around his neck. And so, after Joachim's return, the text observes that the couple rested the first day in their house. We are to understand from the next chapter that it was during this interlude that the conception of Mary took place. The term 'rested' likely refers to the sabbath (Genesis 2:3, NJB).

4.4.b. Anna's vow is that her child will be a nazirite, dedicated to God, holy to God, and to serve him 'all the days of its life'. In comparison, Samson will be a nazirite from the day of his birth and Samuel from his third year after he was brought to the temple at Shiloh. Anna's vow is more extensive and involves the conception of Mary.

> Antiphon. O Lord I have heard of your renown, and I stand in awe, O Lord, of your work. In our own time revive it; in our own time make it known; in wrath may you remember mercy. God comes from Teman, the Holy One from Mount Paran. His glory covered the heavens, and the earth was full of his praise. The brightness was like the sun; rays came forth from his hand, where his power lay hidden. He stopped and shook the earth; he looked and made the nations tremble. The eternal mountains were shattered; among his ancient pathways the everlasting hills sank low. (Habakkuk 3:2–4, 6).

According to the basic chronology followed here, Jesus was born c. 5 BCE. Subtracting 9 months for the gestation of Jesus and 12 years since the birth of Mary (8.2) then Mary would have been born c. 18 BCE.

The Second Temple period, 516 BCE–70 CE, includes the time of Herod's rebuilding of the temple between 25 BCE–19 BCE, and its dedication in 18 BCE. Religious worship and temple rituals continued during the construction period.[24]

---

[24] See, Wikipedia, 'Second Temple'.

As a result, Mary's conception and the dedication of the temple after Herod's reconstruction took place at approximately the same time.

> Antiphon. For I am about to create new heavens and a new earth; the former things shall not be remembered or come to mind. But be glad and rejoice for ever in what I am creating; for I am about to create Jerusalem as a joy, and its people as a delight. (Isaiah 65:17–18)

The Protevangelium of James, Chapter 5

The Birth of Mary

5.1   The next day he brought his offering, saying to himself, "If the Lord God is gracious to me the [golden] plate of the [high] priest will make it clear to me." And Joachim brought his offerings and observed attentively the [high] priest's plate when he went up to the altar of the Lord and he saw no stain in himself. And Joachim said, "Now I know that the Lord is gracious to me and has forgiven me all my sins." And he came down from the temple of the Lord justified and returned to his house.

5.2   And her months were fulfilled; and in the ninth month Anna gave birth. And she said to the midwife, "What have I brought forth?" And she said, "A girl." And Anna said, "My soul has been magnified this day." And she lay down. Now, when her days were fulfilled, Anna purified herself and gave suck to the child and called her name Mary.

Commentary

5.1.a.   Anna and Joachim have independently received angelic visitations that prophesy the birth of their child. Joachim is already convinced and is in celebration (4.3) when he gathers a large offering to the Lord in thanksgiving and it arrives by his home just as he himself does. After one night of 'rest' with Anna, he goes to the temple to make his offering. Amann thinks that Joachim believes that by watching the [high] priest's plate he may detect any sign of sin in him. Amann dismisses this concept but at the same time he does not understand what is happening.

The relevant information is based on a text from Exodus.

> Antiphon. You shall make a rosette of pure gold, and engrave on it, like the engraving of a signet, "Holy to the Lord." You shall fasten it on the turban with a blue cord; it shall be on the front of the turban. It shall be on Aaron's forehead, and Aaron shall take on himself any guilt incurred in the holy offering that the Israelites consecrate as their sacred donations; it shall always be on his forehead, in order that they may find favor before the Lord. (Exodus 28:36–38).

In his analysis, Amann is correct in recognizing that the 'plate' on the priests forehead is suspended from the high priest's turban. For a rich and generous man such as Joachim, with a long history of bringing a double portion of his offerings to the temple (1.1) it is not surprising that the high priest is there. He would have heard of the controversy in the temple and of Joachim's flight to the wilderness and he knows of his return. He has likely also had information from Anna, through his sources, and when Joachim suddenly shows up immediately after he returns then the high priest would likely want to see him.

5.1.b. The plate itself functioned to remove any sin that the people were guilty of when offering sacrifice. It was not regarded as something purely symbolic but as something functional. Evidently, it attracted to itself the stain that accrued in the innermost sanctuary from tainted offerings, and it allowed that stain to be removed.[25] Therefore, when Joachim brought his offerings he closely observed the high priest's plate. When he saw that there was no stain there he concluded that there was no guilt in him. Amann misunderstands the ritual; even if a stain had appeared on the plate, the offering would be purified and therefore would be rendered acceptable to the Lord.

Joachim did not acquire certainty that his sins were forgiven. Rather, he acquired the awareness that he was without sin in the first place. Any former sins that he may have committed had already been forgiven him. In seeing no guilt in himself, Joachim was exonerated. Any doubts that had arisen in his mind from Reuben's rudeness had fled. The public rebuke that he should not 'be first among those who bring offerings' (1.2) because he did not have the blessing of children was unwarranted.

It is also misleading to say that Joachim acquired certainty that the infertility of his wife was going to cease. This was already a done deed. The thrust of the narrative is that his wife had already conceived the night before following Joachim's return (4.4).

5.1.c. On his return home from the temple, Joachim felt 'justified' but the reason for this has nothing to do with the chain of thought of Amann (1910:197) or the argument of Hock (1995:41, fn. 5.4) who made a similar argument. Joachim did not bring his offerings with a prayer for God's mercy. The narrative makes it clear that he brought them in gratitude for a blessing that he had received. He also made use of the occasion to verify his own righteousness. The sense of justification that Joachim feels is best explained by a psalm.

(Psalm 66:10–20)

> For you, O God, have tested us; you have tried us as silver is tried.
> You brought us into the net; you laid burdens on our backs;
> you let people ride over our heads; we went through fire and through water;
> yet you have brought us out to a spacious place.
> I will come into your house with burnt offerings;
> I will pay you my vows, those that my lips uttered and my mouth promised when I was in trouble.
> I will offer to you burnt offerings of fatlings, with the smoke of the sacrifice of rams;
> I will make an offering of bulls and goats. Selah
> Come and hear, all you who fear God, and I will tell what he has done for me.
> I cried aloud to him, and he was extolled with my tongue.

---

[25] Richard J. Clifford and Roland E. Murphy, "Exodus," in *The New Jerome Biblical Commentary* (Englewood Cliffs, New Jersey, 1990), 57.

> If I had cherished iniquity in my heart, the Lord would not have listened.
> But truly God has listened; he has given heed to the words of my prayer.
> Blessed be God, because he has not rejected my prayer or removed his steadfast love from me.

The Protevangelium gives no indication of any miraculous event during the entire time of Anna's pregnancy. Amann (1910:197) includes this comment because of later recensions in which a number of miraculous events during Anna's pregnancy are mentioned.

5.2.a.   After a normal pregnancy of nine months, Anna gives birth. Some copyists have thought it better for Mary to be born premature and have substituted the seventh or the eighth month for the ninth. But these copies are suspect. In the Byzantine literature one finds protests against the idea that it was more suitable for the dignity of Mary to be born early. (Amann, 1910:198). See also, Hock, 1995:43, fn. 5:5.

5.2.b.   For Anna, the suspense about the sex of her child is only resolved when she asks the midwife, 'What have I brought forth?' When she hears it is a girl, she is delighted and proclaims that her 'soul has been magnified'. This last comment is unusual, equivalent to the priest's blessing in (7.3). It indicates that Anna has an inspiration that in her daughter, 'the Lord will manifest his redemption to the children of Israel' (7.3)'.

> Antiphon. Speak to the people of Israel, saying: If a woman conceives and bears a male child, she shall be ceremonially unclean seven days; as at the time of her menstruation, she shall be unclean. On the eighth day the flesh of his foreskin shall be circumcised. Her time of blood purification shall be thirty-three days; she shall not touch any holy thing, or come into the sanctuary, until the days of her purification are completed. If she bears a female child, she shall be unclean two weeks, as in her menstruation; her time of blood purification shall be sixty-six days. (Leviticus 12:1–5).

After her periods of uncleanness and purification, Anna 'gave suck to the child' and 'called her name Mary'. These details are important because the text implies that Mary was tended to by a caregiver until Anna was able to take over. This is associated with the fact that Mary is to be 'holy to the Lord' all the days of her life and this includes the time just after she was born.

In naming Mary, Anna uses a Semitic phrase because she 'called her name Mary', rather than simply 'call her Mary'. The attention to such details may suggest something of the antiquity of the document.

Mary is Blessed by the Priests of the Temple

6.1   Day by day the child grew strong. When she was six months old, her mother set her on the ground to see if she could stand. And having walked seven steps, she returned to her mother's lap. And she lifted her up, saying, "As the Lord my God lives, you shall tread no more upon this earth until I bring you to the temple of the Lord." And she made a sanctuary in her bedroom and did not let anything common or unclean into it. And she called the undefiled daughters of the Hebrews and they entertained her.

6.2   When the child was a year old, Joachim made a great feast. He invited the priests, and the scribes, and the elders and all the people of Israel. And Joachim presented the child to the priests and they blessed her, saying, "O God of our fathers, bless this child and give her an illustrious name for ever in all generations." And all the people said, "So be it, so be it. Amen." And he presented her to the high priests and they blessed her, saying, "O God Most High, look upon this child and bless her with the utmost blessing, which shall be for ever."

6.3   And her mother carried her into the sanctuary of her bedroom and gave her suck. And Anna sang a song to the Lord God, saying:

"I will sing a song to the Lord my God,
    for he has visited me
    and removed from me the reproach of my enemies.
And the Lord gave me the fruit of righteousness,
    singular in its kind
    yet richly endowed before him.
Who will proclaim to the sons of Reuben
    that Anna gives suck?
Hear, hear, O twelve tribes of Israel,
    that Anna gives suck!"
And she laid her to rest in the sanctuary of her bedchamber and went out and served them. When the feast was ended, they went down rejoicing and glorifying the God of Israel.

Commentary

6.1.a.   A few episodes from the infancy of Mary are demonstrated to confirm that Mary followed the priestly code of holiness. Although she was an infant, her mother Anna was responsible to ensure that necessary practices were followed.

At six months of age, Anna put Mary on the ground to see if she could stand. Surprisingly, Mary not only stood but she left her mother and took seven steps (a ritual number). She then stopped and returned to her mother's lap. It was not because her strength failed her but because the demonstration was sufficient. It is enough for Anna to decide that Mary needed to be sheltered from playing in the dirt. This was to preserve her holiness until she was presented to the temple of the Lord. It is not about inappropriate behavior in one so young, but Mary must follow the priestly code of holiness since she is a nazirite. The temple regulations regarding ritual purity were to be imposed upon her because she is consecrated to the Lord. Anna had the responsibility to see that it was done.

Mary has given proof of her precocity and Anna feared about her wandering about here and there to the detriment of her holiness. Since, from before her birth, she had been consecrated to the service of God, it was necessary to separate her from anything that might defile her according to the priestly code. This is what prompted Anna to create a sanctuary for Mary in her bedroom and she would not let anything 'common or unclean' into it. She also called the 'undefiled daughters of the Hebrews' to entertain Mary.

6.1.b. The Greek word used for the room set aside for Mary is translated as "sanctuary." This is the usual translation of the term when it occurs, almost exclusively, in biblical and Christian literature. It signifies a sacred space that is kept ritually pure. Megan Nutzman provides several examples of its usage.[26] In particular, the term is used seven times in the description of the sacking of Jerusalem and the looting of the temple by Antiochus IV Epiphanes. The issue here is the pollution and desecration of the temple, which Antiochus effected not only by taking its treasures but also by shedding innocent blood. (Nutzman, 2013:567).

> He arrogantly entered the sanctuary and took the golden altar, the lampstand for the light, and all its utensils. (1 Maccabees 1:21).

> They stored up arms and food, and collecting the spoils of Jerusalem they stored them there, and became a great menace, for the citadel became an ambush against the sanctuary, an evil adversary of Israel at all times. On every side of the sanctuary they shed innocent blood; they even defiled the sanctuary. (1 Maccabees 1: 35–37).

> Her sanctuary became desolate like a desert; her feasts were turned into mourning … (1 Maccabees 1:39).

> … he directed them to follow customs strange to the land, to forbid burnt offerings and sacrifices and drink offerings in the sanctuary, to profane sabbaths and festivals, to defile the sanctuary and the priests. (1 Maccabees 1:44–46).).

The term sanctuary used in (6.1) emphasizes that Mary's retreat was a true sanctuary in which Anna 'did not permit anything common or unclean to pass through it' and that it was maintained in a state of ritual purity. This is a law for nazirites, and Anna had to be careful about it since Mary was dedicated to God and was holy to God for all the days of her life, and this included her infancy.

[26] Megan Nutzman, "Mary in the *Protevangelium of James:* A Jewish Woman in the Temple?" in *Greek, Roman, and Byzantine Studies* 53, 2013, 551–578.

6.1.c.   To maintain the holiness of Mary's surroundings, Anna is particular not only about Mary's food, but also about her companions (Nutzman, 2013:569). It is in the context of Mary's sanctuary and its carefully protected ritual purity that one first meets 'the undefiled daughters of the Hebrews'. The use of the definite article presupposes that these girls are an identifiable group. They will reappear in (7.2) and are characterized as being "undefiled" – the same distinction given to the virgin weavers of the temple veils and to Mary herself in (10.1).

Scholars have frequently challenged the very existence of a group such as 'the undefiled daughters of the Hebrews' and have argued that there is no evidence for such a group (Hock, 1995:43, fn. 6:5). This is unfortunate since there is evidence.

Nutzman, 2013:569–570, argues that the text designates a single group of undefiled virgins although the references in (6.1) and (7.2) "make no mention of their work on the curtains." She infers that the text envisioned a company of virgins, whose existence as a discrete group extended beyond their responsibilities to construct the temple curtains."

Saul Lieberman, drawing upon rabbinic sources that will be looked at in more detail in chapter 8, argues that "the undefiled daughters of the Hebrews" are young girls who did weaving in the temple. He notes that a commentary on the tractate Tamid 29b, ascribed to RABAD, explains that these "girls did not reach the age of puberty (*menses muliebres*), and were consequently ritually pure."[27] He concludes that the use of "undefiled" in (6.1) is the Greek translation of a technical phrase in Hebrew that meant "virgins who have not yet menstruated." He believes that its use in the Protevangelium "was probably taken from a well-informed Jewish source" (Lieberman, 1950:168).

The undefiled virgins are young, for once they have reached the age of puberty – approximately twelve years old –their menstrual flow when it came would compromise the ritual purity of the temple. The question is one of contamination, which pollutes both the sacrifice and the sanctuary itself (Nutzman, 2013:568, fn. 37. This notion of menstrual pollution is an ancient one found in the Old Testament.

> Antiphon. When a woman has a discharge of blood that is her regular discharge from her body, she shall be in her impurity for seven days, and whoever touches her shall be unclean until the evening. Everything upon which she lies during her impurity shall be unclean; everything also upon which she sits shall be unclean. Whoever touches her bed shall wash his clothes, and bathe in water, and be unclean until the evening. Whoever touches anything upon which she sits shall wash his clothes, and bathe in water, and be unclean until the evening; whether it is the bed or anything upon which she sits, when he touches it he shall be unclean until the evening. If any man lies with her, and her impurity falls on him, he shall be unclean for seven days; and every bed on which he lies shall be unclean. (Leviticus 15:19–24).

The final phrase 'they entertained her' in (6.1) has bedeviled interpreters but as pointed out by Meyer, 1904, it can be explained by a late meaning of the Greek word that corresponds exactly to the Latin *divertere* from which comes the French *divertir*, "to entertain." Interestingly, this particular meaning was also understood in

---

[27] Saul Lieberman, *Hellenism in Jewish Palestine*. New York, 1950:167, esp. fn. 30.

the ancient Syriac version (Amann, 1910:201). Comments such as this indicate the value of having such a fifth century manuscript.

From the point of view of narrative development, the invitation to have the undefiled daughters of the Hebrews entertain Mary also provides an unofficial link to the temple. The select group of virgins, as well as entertaining Mary, are able to monitor her fulfillment of the vow made by Anna. They provide a first point of contact with the priests from the temple. They are aware of Mary and are keeping track of her.

6.2.a.   When Mary is one year old, Joachim had a great feast to introduce her to the priesthood. It has been suggested that the celebration of Mary's birthday is a narrative device by which the child is initially introduced to the priesthood (Amann (1910:112). However, the entire reason for the feast is to introduce Mary to the priesthood. There is no celebration of the age of Mary; she just happened to be one year old when the feast is held.

Many people have been invited to the feast, but the only purpose of it is to introduce Mary to the group of priests and to the group of high priests. They are aware of Anna's vow and that Mary has been dedicated to the Lord. They have sent undefiled daughters of the Hebrews to entertain her and almost certainly to monitor her. Now the priests will see Mary for the first time and they will bless her.

6.2.b.   Joachim first introduces Mary to the priests. The group of priests then bless her in unison and appear to use a ritual blessing.

'O God of our fathers, bless this child and give her an illustrious name forever in all generations'. The crowd responded: 'So be it, so be it. Amen'.

Joachim then introduced Mary to the high priests. They also bless her in unison and also appear to use a ritual blessing.

'O God Most High, look upon this child and bless her with the utmost blessing, which shall be for ever.'

The present translation uses 'God Most High' in the preceding statement. Amann (1910) suggests 'God of the Heights' and Elliott (2022) suggests 'God of the heavenly heights' but neither are used as divine names in the Old Testament. Hock (1995) suggests 'Most high God' which is a variant of the accepted title and Walker (1886) suggests 'God Most High' and notes it is common in the Old Testament, and not dissimilar to the other translations. A significant fact not mentioned is that the divine name, 'Most High' also appears in (11.3).

Amann (1910:202) notes that the Syriac understands the blessing of the high priest to be "a blessing that never ends".

6.3.a.   Following the blessings of the priests and high priests, Anna takes Mary into the sanctuary of her bedroom and gave her suck. And Anna sang a song to the Lord.

The translation of Anna's song follows Amann but is influenced by Walker (1886). The prelude, 'I will sing a song to the Lord my God', recalls the introduction to certain psalms (Psalm 96:1, 149:1).

The blessings that Mary received from the priests and high priests had removed any hurt that she had personally endured, 'for he has visited me and removed from me the reproach of my enemies'.

Amann (1910:203) suggests that this recalls Rachel giving birth to her first son.

> Antiphon. Then God remembered Rachel, and God heeded her and opened her womb. She conceived and bore a son, and said, 'God has taken away my reproach; and she named him Joseph'. (Genesis 30:22–24).

This leads back to the historical incident of how Reuben was supplanted by Joseph who gained the birthright of Jacob. Anna's song relates her own story to that of Rachel who bore Joseph and is the matriarch of the house of David from whom shall come the Messiah. It appears that Anna is identifying with Rachel as her matriarch.

The continuation of Anna's song is in full agreement with the words, 'and the Lord gave me the fruit of righteousness, singular in its kind yet richly endowed before him' (Amann, 1910:124). The fruit of righteousness is certified by many manuscripts, including the Syriac, and is more natural than the 'fruit of his righteousness' maintained by Tischendorf and echoed in Hock, 1995:45, fn. 6:12. The present translation follows the ancient Syriac manuscript. The words in Anna's song come from a messianic prophecy of Isaiah.

> Antiphon. Then justice will dwell in the wilderness, and righteousness abide in the fruitful field. The effect of righteousness will be peace, and the result of righteousness, quiet and trust for ever. (Isaiah 32:16–17).

This then reflects the blessing that the high priests gave to Mary, 'the utmost blessing, which shall be for ever'. Anna's song shows that Mary had received a messianic blessing from the high priests.

The ending of Anna's song, 'Who will proclaim to the sons of Reuben that Anna gives suck? Hear, hear, O twelve tribes of Israel, that Anna gives suck!', recalls the words of Sarah.

This also appears to be a defiant song of Anna that she is of the house of David and Rachel is her matriarch.

> Antiphon. And she said, 'Who would ever have said to Abraham that Sarah would nurse children? Yet I have borne him a son in his old age.' (Genesis 21:7).

The Reuben in Anna's song is the eldest son of Jacob. A distant descendant of him, represented by his namesake, is the person who insulted Joachim in the temple.

The song of Anna is a defiant messianic song. The high priests at the feast participated in a messianic blessing for Mary. The priests are showing that they are actively involved in the story of Mary. And they appear to believe that Mary will have a role in the messianic age.

Anna, after putting Mary to bed, then went out and served the guests. When the feast ended, they went down rejoicing and glorifying God.

The priests and high priests have approved of Mary with blessings and Anna's song does the same. When the feast is over, 'they went down rejoicing and glorifying the God of Israel.' The language is significant since one 'goes up' or 'comes down' in relation to the holiness of the location to which one is going to or from which one is coming. For example, in (5.1), Joachim 'went up to the altar of the Lord' and later ' came down from the temple of the Lord'. The text shows that the priests and others attending the feast implicitly recognize the holiness of the sanctuary of Mary. It is a sign that the temple approves of Mary's vocation, and they appear to see it in messianic terms. When the time comes, the temple will welcome Mary.

6.3.b.   The final section of Ezekiel:40–48 presents a blueprint for the religious and political rehabilitation of the Israelite nation in Palestine. The priestly system is grounded in Ezekiel's program and the temple ritual in all its detail is based upon the sacerdotal view of holiness. It is into this holiness framework that Mary has been inserted.

The system counts ten degrees of holiness for a variety of places and an understanding of it is helpful in studying the Protevangelium. The degrees of holiness with regard to the temple and its precincts are indicated by the imposition of ever-increasing restrictions regarding who may enter into its various parts.

> 1.6   There are ten degrees of holiness. The Land of Israel is holier than all other lands. And what is its holiness? People bring the omer [barley] offering, and the bikurim [first fruits] offering, and the two loaves from there. These cannot be brought from any other land.

> 1.7   The walled cities [of the Land of Israel, from the period of Joshua] are still more holy because people had to send away the metzoraim [lepers] from their midst, and they may carry a corpse therein [to its burial place] as far as necessary, but once it is taken out, they may not bring it back.

> 1.8   Inside the wall [of Jerusalem] is more holy than these, because there they may eat of the lesser holy sacrifices and the second tithe. The Temple Mount has greater sanctity, because men and women with discharges, menstruating women, and women who have given birth] may not enter there. The outer wall of the Temple courtyard has higher sanctity, because gentiles and people contaminated with corpse impurity may not enter there. The Court of Women has higher sanctity, because a tevul yom [someone who had only become ritually pure on that very day] may not enter there, but they are not liable for a sin offering for doing so. The Court of the Israelites has higher sanctity, because one whose atonement is incomplete may not enter there, and is liable for a sin offering for doing so. The Court of the Priests has higher sanctity, because the Israelites [that is, non-kohanim] may not enter there except at the time of their [ritual] requirements: the laying on of hands, the slaughter, and the wave-offering [an elevation].

1.9 [The area] between the Hall and the Altar has still higher sanctity, because [priests] with blemishes and loosened hair [bareheaded] may not enter there. The Sanctuary has higher sanctity, because no one may enter there who has not washed their hands and feet. The Holy of Holies has greater sanctity than [all of] these, because no one may enter there except the High Priest on the Day of Atonement at the time of the service.

(Mishnah Kelim 1:6–9)

The Lord God Sends his Grace upon Mary

7.1   The months passed and were added to the child. And the child was two years old, and Joachim said, "Let us take her up to the temple of the Lord, so that we may fulfill the promise that we have made, lest the Lord claim it of us and render our offering unacceptable." And Anna said, "Let us wait for the third year so that the child may no more long for her father or mother." And Joachim said, "Let us wait."

7.2   And the child was three years old, and Joachim said, "Call the undefiled daughters of the Hebrews and ask each to take a lamp. And let them stand with their lamps burning so that the child may not turn back, and her heart be tempted away from the temple of the Lord." And they did so until they had gone up to the temple of the Lord.

7.3   And the priest received her, and embraced her, and blessed her, saying, "The Lord has magnified your name in all generations. Through you, in the last days, the Lord will manifest his redemption to the children of Israel."

7.4   And he placed her on the third step of the altar, and the Lord God sent his grace upon her, and she danced with her feet, and the whole house of Israel loved her.

Commentary

7.1.a.   The child Mary was two years old, and Joachim thought to fulfill the promise made in the vow of Anna and bring her to the temple. He feared that if they delayed, the Lord would be angry (Amann, 1910:204). The simplest way to understand this is that if they fulfill their vow then God will not have a claim against them and as a result their offering would be more pleasing to God.

Anna interrupted and said that they should not do so yet but 'wait for the third year'. She explained that at this time their 'child may no more long for her father and mother'. This is a delicate response describing the weaning of Mary. Joachim understood the observation and gave his consent.

In this action, Mary is rephrasing the concern of Hannah when she felt it was too early to bring Samuel to the temple.

> Antiphon. But Hannah did not go up, for she said to her husband, 'As soon as the child is weaned, I will bring him, that he may appear in the presence of the Lord, and remain there forever; I will offer him as a

nazirite for all time.' Her husband Elkanah said to her, 'Do what seems best to you, wait until you have weaned him; only – may the Lord establish his word.' So the woman remained and nursed her son, until she weaned him. (1 Samuel 1:22–23).

Elkanah is concerned about Hannah's vow – just as Joachim is concerned about Anna's vow – and uses the phrase ' may the Lord establish his word' to indicate that the word of the Lord that Hannah had received should be accomplished. Joachim understood Anna's word in the same way, and he consented.

Based on their decision, Mary would be brought to the temple in her third year. The age of three, may be a symbolic time for weaning as suggested by the decisions of Hannah and Anna. This same age for weaning is also found in 2 Maccabees, in passing, for a mother who mentions it.

> Antiphon. My son, have pity on me. I carried you for nine months in my womb, and nursed you for three years, and have reared you and brought you up to this point in your life, and have taken care of you. (2 Maccabees 7:27).

7.1.b. In these early stories in the narrative, there is a weaving of details that occur in the Old Testament antecedents from the stories of Samson and Samuel.

Like the mother of Samson, Anna received an angelic visitation before she conceived; she vowed to make her child a nazirite all the days of her life. She maintained ritual purity for her child and would not let anything common or unclean enter Mary's sanctuary.

Like Hannah and the mother of Samson, Anna has a natural conception after a period of sterility.

Like Hannah, Anna made a nazirite vow before her child was conceived; her husband agreed to keep Mary until she was weaned; Mary is brought to the temple in her third year (or weaned).

The stories of Anna and Joachim are based on prominent antecedents in the Old Testament. First among these are stories involving Samson's mother and two of Anna's namesakes: (Anna and Tobias) and (Hannah and Elkanah). Joachim also has his own namesake.

The story of Mary begins much as the story of Samson's mother, with the exception that Anna's vow preempts the angelic visitor on behalf of her future child. To interrupt an angelic visitation – rather than simply participate in it – indicates that the spontaneous assertion of Anna results from a prophetic revelation and it includes the unusual assertion that the vow concerning her child is going to apply for 'all the days of its life'. This would include the conception of the child, and greatly exceeds the vow for Samson, ' from his birth', and the vow for Samuel 'until he is presented to the Lord after his weaning'. This vow of Anna is remarkable, and it would be noted by the priests.

The blending of the stories of the classical nazirites into a seamless model for the story of Mary reinforces the identification of Anna's vow as a nazirite vow. Their stories intersect with Mary's story. They prefigure Mary, who is holy to the Lord. It is through such stories that the narrative speaks to the truth of Mary, a Mary rooted in the Old Testament and a Mary of unusual holiness.

Some aspects of the narrative are unique to Mary, as in the messianic blessing of the high priests (6.2) and in Anna's messianic song placing Mary within the history of Israel (6.3).

7.2.a. When Mary is in her third year, Joachim brings up the necessity of fulfilling Anna's vow that she had made for Mary. They called the 'undefiled daughters of the Hebrews', the girls who had started visiting Mary in (6.2), to come with burning lamps and lead her to the temple so that she might not be tempted to turn back. And they did that until they had arrived at the temple of the Lord. Joachim was realistic that this would distract Mary from turning back and knew that the girls who had been visiting Mary for two and a half years would be her companions when she began her new life in the temple.

7.3.a. It appears that only one priest received Mary at the temple. He embraced her and blessed her with an invocation similar to what the priests said during Mary's presentation to the priests in (6.2). When Mary was one year old, the priests asked God to 'give her an illustrious name forever in all generations'. Now, at three years old, it appears to have been accomplished for 'the Lord has magnified your name in all generations'. The priest is not done with his prophecy for he adds that it is through Mary, 'in the last days', that 'the Lord will manifest his redemption to the children of Israel'. Mary is identified as the one who will have an important role in the coming of the messianic age.

The message is remarkable because of the focus on Mary for she is now involved in the dawn of the messianic age. Given Old Testament beliefs, it appears that the priests are thinking that Mary may be the mother of the Messiah. By implication, they would think of Mary as being of the house of David. The reference to 'the last days' is a sign that the messianic age is getting closer.

7.4.a. As often happens in the Old Testament, prophecies are not only through words but also through enactments.

> *And he placed her on the third step of the altar*

This action begins a prophetic encounter involving Mary. It is also one of the most perplexing statements in the Protevangelium because Mary is holy to the Lord and would not transgress the holiness law of the temple.

After the Babylonian exile, the Second Temple was inaugurated in Jerusalem, about 516 BCE. In its last phase, it was enhanced by Herod the Great, the result later being referred to as Herod's Temple. The Second Temple was eventually destroyed in 70 CE.

In the present historiography, the inauguration of Herod's Temple took place at approximately the time that Mary was born. Since Mary is now in her third year, then the present episode and all later episodes in the Protevangelium take place in this phase of the Second Temple.

Amann, discussed the holiness issue about placing Mary on the third step of the altar, but is also puzzled as to why the episode is described in such a straightforward way. He knew that the altar of sacrifice in Herod's Temple, had a large ramp around the altar and that it had no steps. He also recognized that the altar in Ezekiel's prophetic description of the New Temple did have steps. Ezekiel 43:13–17, provides the details with the final comment stating that 'its steps shall face east'.[28]

Given that the altar in (7.3) had steps and the current altar in the earthly temple did not, then what is happening here is not related to the current earthly temple. The law of holiness pertaining to the altar in the temple is not involved because the action takes place in the vision of the New Temple. If one turns to the vision of the New Temple, described in Ezekiel 40–48, it is described by a heavenly architect, 'whose appearance shone like bronze, with a linen cord and a measuring reed in his hand' (Ezekiel 40:3). It too is a vision of God's heavenly temple upon the earth. In this case, the altar in question in Ezekiel's vision is a replica of the "true altar" in the heavenly temple.

The language that Ezekiel uses is similar to the language that Moses used in creating the first tabernacle.

> Antiphon. And have them make me a sanctuary, so that I may dwell among them. In accordance with all that I show you concerning the pattern of the tabernacle and of all its furniture, so you shall make it. (Exodus 25:8–9).

> Antiphon. And see that you make them according to the pattern for them, which is being shown you on the mountain. (Exodus 25:40).

The action of the priest prophetically places Mary on the third step of Ezekiel's altar, an altar yet to be built, a replica of the heavenly altar. Mary then faces east since she is on the third step of the altar which faces east. She experiences Ezekiel's vision of the glory of God returning to the temple through the east gate.

> Antiphon. Then he brought me to the gate, the gate facing east. And there the glory of the God of Israel was coming from the east; the sound was like the sound of mighty waters; and the earth shone with his glory. … As the glory of the Lord entered the temple by the gate facing east, the spirit lifted me up, and brought me into the inner court; and the glory of the Lord filled the temple. (Ezekiel 43:1–2, 4–5).

When Mary enters the vision, she sees what Ezekiel saw.

7.4.b. *And the Lord God sent his grace upon her*

> the glory of the God of Israel
> > the sound of mighty waters
> > > earth shining with his glory
> > > > the glory of the Lord filling the temple

---

[28] Amann, 1910:135; Hoch 1995:45, fn. 7:9.

In this encounter, Mary is welcomed by God in the heavenly temple since the encounter in Ezekiel's vision is a prophetic one and this encounter shows the 'glory of God' welcoming Mary in the heavenly temple.

7.4.c.   *and she danced with her feet*

Mary danced because the Ark of God would be returning to Jerusalem.

> Antiphon. David and all the house of Israel were dancing before the Lord with all their might, with songs and lyres and harps and tambourines and castanets and cymbals. (2 Samuel 6:5).

7.4.d.   *and the whole house of Israel loved her*

This expresses the joy of Israel because of the coming of the messianic age and Mary's role in it. At the present time, this is simply an expectation.

The Protevangelium will say that Mary lived in the heavenly holy of holies. This does not mean that she lived in heaven because she lived on earth. However, she did have spiritual access to God for 'the Lord God sent his grace upon her'. This 'grace' is her spiritual presence in the heavenly holy of holies for it is through Mary that God will find a 'resting place' on earth.

> Antiphon. Thus says the Lord: Heaven is my throne and the earth is my footstool; what is the house that you would build for me, and what is my resting place? (Isaiah 66:1).

7. Supplemental. Many commentators have felt that having such young people associated with the temple as in the case of Mary is unwarranted. Nevertheless, more evidence on this will be given in chapter 10. For the moment, it is significant that rabbinical sources indicate that some children were raised in conditions of strict ritual purity – as was the case with Mary – in order that the temple might employ them in a future service.

> Antiphon. Our Rabbis taught: The women who brought up their children for the [services of the red] heifer, received their wages from the Temple funds. Abba Saul said: The notable women of Jerusalem fed them and maintained them. (B. Kethuboth 106a).

In an explanation of this, the following comment is attached.

> Antiphon. Cf. Num. 19.2ff. Certain services in connection with its preparation had to be entrusted to children who from birth were brought up under conditions of scrupulous ritual purity. For this purpose, the mothers had to live in specially constructed buildings from the ante-natal period until the time the children were ready for their duties. (Cf. Sukkah 21a).

The above information says that ritual purity had to be maintained from the time before birth until the children were old enough to be ready for their duties. The Protevangelium is scrupulous with respect to such a stricture in the discussion of Mary up until the point she was brought to the temple. This rabbinic tradition suggests that it is plausible that other groups, such as the "virgin weavers" to be encountered in chapter 10 may also have been prepared for duties associated with the temple, as were the "red heifer" children.[29]

---

29 This same point has been made by Saul Lieberman, *Hellenism in Jewish Palestine*, New York, 1950, 168, fn. 33.

Mary in the Temple at Age 12

8.1   And her parents went down marveling and praising the Lord God, because the child had not turned back. And Mary was in the temple of the Lord as if she were a dove that dwelt there, and she received food from the hand of an angel.

8.2   And when she was twelve years old, there took place a council of the priests. They said, "Behold, Mary has reached the age of twelve years in the temple of the Lord. What then shall we do with her lest perchance she defiles the sanctuary of the Lord?" And they said to the high priest, "You stand at the altar of the Lord. Go into the sanctuary and pray concerning her. Whatever the Lord reveals to you, that also we will do."

8.3   And the high priest, wearing the vestment with the twelve bells, went into the Holy of Holies and prayed concerning her. And behold, an angel of the Lord appeared, saying to him, "Zechariah, Zechariah, go out and assemble the widowers of the people. Let each of them bring a staff and to whomsoever the Lord shall show a sign, then she shall be his wife." And the heralds went out, through all the country about Judea, and the trumpet of the Lord sounded, and all came running.

Commentary

8.1.a.   Mary's parents went down from the temple, expressing surprise and praising the Lord God because Mary had not turned back. Since Anna had vowed that Mary would be a nazirite all the days of her life, dedicated to God, to be holy to the Lord, and to be a servant of God, a crucial moment had passed. She was now in the hands of the temple. Joachim and Anna remembered the joy they felt when she was born and the time that she had spent with them. But now, Mary would live her life that had been promised to the Lord. Joachim and Anna now disappear from the narrative.

8.1.b.   Mary's life for the next several years is to live in the temple of the Lord as though she were a dove that dwelt there, and she received food from the hand of an angel.

> Antiphon. And I say, 'O that I had wings like a dove! I would fly away and be at rest; truly, I would flee far away; I would lodge in the wilderness; I would hurry to find shelter for myself from the raging wind and tempest.' (Psalm 55:6–8).

In (6.2), when Mary was one year old, she received a blessing from the high priests: 'O God Most High look upon this child and bless her with the utmost blessing, which shall be forever' Now that she is 3 years old, she need not fly away for shelter, since she is living in the temple of the Lord.

> Antiphon. You who live in the shelter of the Most High, who abide in the shadow of the Almighty will say to the Lord, 'My refuge and my fortress; my God in whom I trust.' (Psalm 91:1–2).

Mary was 'a dove that dwelt there'.

> Antiphon. He will cover you with his pinions, and under his wings you will find refuge; his faithfulness is a shield and buckler. (Psalm 91:4).

Mary 'received food from the hand of an angel'.

> Antiphon. Because you have made the Lord your refuge , the Most High your dwelling place, no evil shall befall you, no scourge come near your tent. For he will command his angels concerning you to guard you in all your ways. On their hands they will bear you up, so that you will not dash your foot against a stone. (Psalm 91:10–12).

The psalm describes Mary as not someone living in heaven but as someone who lives in the temple on earth and is under the protection of God.

8.2.a.   The stay of Mary in the temple had to be ended soon after Mary became 12 years old, The priests had to decide what they must do with her lest she might defile the sanctuary of the Lord. The age of 12 was chosen because it gave a sufficient time of safety before the beginning of the first period of Mary. A woman with a period would generate a blood defilement in the temple, and this was taken very seriously.

> Antiphon. When a woman has a discharge of blood that is her regular discharge from her body, she shall be in her impurity for seven days, and whoever touches her shall be unclean until the evening. Everything upon which she lies during her impurity shall be unclean; everything also upon which she sits shall be unclean. Whoever touches her bed shall wash his clothes, and bathe in water, and be unclean until the evening. Whoever touches anything upon which she sits shall wash his clothes, and bathe in water, and be unclean until the evening; whether it is the bed or anything upon which she sits, when he touches it he shall be unclean until the evening. If any man lies with her, and her impurity falls on him, he shall be unclean for seven days; and every bed on which he lies shall be unclean. (Leviticus 15:19–24).

When Mary had reached the age of twelve years she had completed her time of service as an undefiled virgin in the temple. Her first menstruation, presumably in the not-too-distant future, and later ones as well, would temporarily exclude her from the temple precincts. According to the prohibition in Leviticus, anyone who came into contact with a menstruant, her bedding, or even the place where she had been sitting would also become ritually unclean.

8.2.b.   In general, scholars have accepted without quibble that the age of twelve is a reasonable estimate for the menarche, or first menstrual bleeding. The question arises as to the accuracy of this estimate and its sufficiency in safeguarding the ritual purity of the temple from young girls undergoing their menarche. From both social and medical perspectives, the menarche is often considered the central event of female puberty, as it signals the possibility of fertility. Leona Zacharias and Richard Wurtman have made the following helpful observations regarding menarche.[30]

> In normal girls evidence of sexual maturation characteristically appear between ten or twelve years of age. At that time, most healthy girls begin to have physical manifestations of the changes in ovarian function that are associated with reproductive maturity. Their breasts start to bud, and hair appears in the pubic and axillary regions. Within a year, the first episode of menstrual bleeding occurs, providing clear evidence that the ovary is now capable of secreting significant quantities of steroid hormones. Sometime thereafter, the brain begins to emit cyclic neuroendocrine signals at intervals of approximately 29 days; these signals cause the pituitary gland to release the hormones responsible for ovulation, and the reproductive capability of a woman is thereby established.
>
> To explain the fluctuations in the age at menarche with time, Fluhmann [in 1958] proposed "… the possibility that there is a uniform, relatively early prototype for the menarcheal age which applies to the whole human race and which becomes delayed as the result of adverse external circumstances."
>
> In summary, the age at onset of menstruation is not fixed, but varies from population to population, and changes with time. Although it is to some extent influenced by family heredity, body build, photic input and season, it seems more susceptible to modification by certain socioeconomic influences (such as nutrition and urban vs rural living) and by specific disorders (for example, diabetes, obesity and blindness).
>
> (Zacharias and Wurtman, "Age at Menarche," 1969:868–875).

Other investigators have examined the literature concerning the long-term secular trends in the age at menarche in Israel during the past century. They excluded some studies if participants had been investigated due to illness or any condition that could affect sexual maturation. The participants in these studies were divided into two cohorts before and after 1970. It was concluded that the age at menarche "varied little among women born between 1875 and 1970, but there was a clear downwards trend from 13.4 in 1970 to 12.8 two decades later."[31]

Given the stability in the age at menarche between 1875 and 1970 in Israel and the fact that socioeconomic influences (such as nutrition and urban versus rural living) after 1970 would tend to lower the age at menarche, the best estimate we can make for the age at menarche in first-century Israel is likely somewhere around 13.4. This is an average and it must be realized that many young girls will have their menarche months earlier.

---

[30] Leona Zacharias and Richard J. Wurtman, "Age at Menarche: Genetic and Environmental Influences," in *New England Journal of Medicine* (April 17), 280, 1969: 868–875.

[31] S. Flash-Luzzatti and others, "Long-term secular trends in the age at menarche in Israel: a systematic literature review and pooled analysis," Epub Feb 5, 2014.

Thus, having the undefiled virgins retire when they turn twelve would provide an adequate buffer for the maintenance of temple purity. There could be outliers, and a virgin weaver might have her menarche before the age of twelve, but such cases would be small in number. On the other hand, if the retirement age was raised, say to thirteen or fourteen, there would be major consequences since the number of virgins defiling the temple would skyrocket. Therefore, the Protevangelium has made a suitable choice for the age of retirement of virgin weavers in the temple.[32]

8.2.c.   The priests said to the high priest, 'you stand at the altar of the Lord' – meaning that he is able to consult the oracle of the Lord – and asked him to go into the sanctuary and pray concerning her (Amann, 1910:212). The priests then agreed to follow whatever was revealed to him.

8.3.a.   The high priest wore the vestment with the twelve bells on the lower hem (Exodus 28: 33–35) when he crossed the sanctuary. The golden bells were to warn people when he was going into or out of the Holy of Holies. Both Josephus (*Antiquities* 3.7.4) and Philo (*Life of Moses* 1.3) speak of them. The number of bells was not determined in the Old Testament. The rabbis spoke of 72 (Amann, 1910:212).

After entering the Holy of Holies, and praying for assistance about Mary, suddenly an angel of the Lord appeared to him and called his name, 'Zecharaiah, Zechariah'. This is the first time that a name has been attributed to a high priest. Amann, 1910:213, observes that the name is applied in all the manuscripts and in all versions (that he knew of at the time). Since this includes the Syriac – the second oldest of all manuscripts – and also Papyrus Bodmer V – the oldest manuscript (see Hock 1995:47, fn. 8:3–9) – the tradition is ancient. Amann also notes that later developments will vary on this tradition, but not the Syriac, and following Hock, not Papyrus Bodmer V.

Zechariah is asked to 'assemble the widowers of the people' where each 'will bring a staff'. Then 'the Lord shall show a sign' and it will assign Mary as a 'wife' to him. There appears to be a hope among the priests, following the narrative so far, that Mary may be a chosen virgin of the house of David who will be the mother of the Messiah. There is no element here of any question pertaining to virginity. The messianic enterprise itself requires a woman of the house of David – assuming matrilineal descent – to have children because one of them may be the Messiah.

The notion that a 'sign' from God will pick the staff of Mary's future husband indicates that whoever is selected will not be known in advance. Only when it occurs, will it be known.

The angelic requirement to summon 'widowers' would be a shock to the high priest for presumably many of the widowers would be older men and this would not conform with his ideas. Yet, the divine oracle is from on high and the high priest must enforce it.

8.3.b.   The heralds went out, throughout Judea, and the trumpet of the Lord sounded, and all came running. They are summoning the widowers.

---

[32] Lieberman, 1950, 168, arrives at the same conclusion but much more succinctly: "But in our case it means virgins who have not reached the age of puberty, a very natural precaution when working on an object of the sanctuary. The virgins were below the age of twelve, the normal age of puberty."

The trumpet of the Lord is the 'shofar', the ram's horn trumpet. It will summon the widowers in Judea as contenders for the hand of Mary.

There are numerous passages in the Old Testament that testify to its use.

> Antiphon. Blow the trumpet at the new moon, at the full moon, on our festal day. For it is a statute for Israel, an ordinance of the God of Jacob. (Psalm 81:3–4).

> Antiphon. So David and all the house of Israel brought up the ark of the Lord with shouting, and with the sound of the trumpet. (2 Samuel 6:15).

And then there is Joel, who advocates blowing the trumpet because the day of the Lord is coming. This is very interesting since Mary has already received a blessing that the Lord has magnified her name in all generations and it is through her, in the last days, that the Lord will manifest his redemption of the children of Israel (7.3).

> Antiphon. Blow the trumpet in Zion; sound the alarm on my holy mountain! Let all the inhabitants of the land tremble, for the day of the Lord is coming, it is near. (Joel 2:1).

Joseph

9.1   And Joseph, getting rid of his adze, went out to join them. And when they were gathered together, they went to the high priest, bringing their staffs with them. He took the staffs from them all, entered into the temple and prayed. Then, having finished his prayer, he took the staffs and went out and returned them. But there was nothing to single out any of them. And Joseph received the last staff, and behold, a dove came out of the rod and flew onto Joseph's head. And the priest said to Joseph, "You have been chosen by lot to take into your care the virgin of the Lord."

9.2   But Joseph refused, saying, "I have children, and I am old while she, she is a child. I am afraid lest I become a laughingstock to the children of Israel." And the priest said to Joseph, "Fear the Lord your God, and remember what God did to Dathan, Abiram, and Korah, how the earth opened and how they were swallowed up because of their rebellion. And now, beware O Joseph, lest the same things happen in your house."

9.3   And Joseph was afraid and took her into his keeping. And Joseph said to Mary, "Behold, I have received you from the temple of the Lord. And now, I leave you in my house and I am off to build my buildings. And I will return to you. (In the meantime) the Lord will protect you.

Commentary

9.1.a.   Joseph is introduced with the sole fact that he put away his adze, indicating that he is a carpenter. He then went out to join the group of contenders, all of whom were carrying a staff. They then went to the high priest and brought their staffs with them. He took all the staffs from them and entered into the temple and prayed. After his prayers, he took the staffs back out and returned them all but there was nothing to single any of them out. Joseph finally received the last staff, and a dove flew out of it and landed on his head.

Then the priest told Joseph that he had been chosen by lot and would take 'into your care the virgin of the Lord'.

The sign of the dove points directly to Mary in the temple for she had already been likened to a dove that dwelt there (8.1). Amann, 1910:215, came to the same conclusion, and so also did Meyer, 1904.

Rather than being appointed as husband of Mary, Joseph is then told to take Mary into his care. The notion is common and different versions give the same idea.

The prodigy having been accomplished, the high priest wants Joseph to accept the role for which he was chosen by the Lord, and he adjusted the command from being a husband to being a guardian.

This is the first time that Mary is referred to as 'the virgin of the Lord' and this ties her to the group formally identified previously as the 'undefiled daughters of the Hebrews' (6.1, 7.2).

9.2.a.   Joseph, however, initially refused, pointing out that he had 'children', he was 'old', and Mary was 'a child'. The Syriac referred to Joseph's male children as being grown men and with some emphasis, on the drawbacks of having fully grown sons in the house of Joseph. This idea is not in the Protevangelium, where Joseph's children are mentioned to emphasize his own age. His children occur in only one place in the Protevangelium. But the narrative suggests that they were mature and did not live in the paternal home (Amann, 1910:217).

What bothers Joseph the most is the obvious discrepancy between his age and that of Mary. The way the high priest responds to this difficulty is peremptory and he threatens Joseph with divine punishment like 'Dathan, Abiram, and Korah' (Numbers 16:27–33).

9.3.   Joseph was afraid and took Mary into his keeping. His fear is based on the issue that God had picked him to care for Mary and he was still struggling with the concept. Inconsistently, with this obligation in his mind, he immediately left for work. Meyer:1904, argued that the absence of Joseph at this critical time was necessary for two narrative reasons: (1) It is necessary to rule out any idea of conjugal relations between Joseph and Mary. (2) It should also leave room for the next chapter and the visit to Elizabeth. Moreover, Joseph was also convinced that the Lord would protect Mary (see 8.1.b).

Mary and the Veil for the Temple

10.1   And there was a council of the priests, saying, "Let us make a veil for the temple of the Lord." And the high priest said, "Call to me the undefiled virgins of the tribe of David." And the officers went and sought and found seven virgins. And the high priest remembered that the child Mary was of the tribe of David and undefiled before God. And the officers went and fetched her.

10.2   And they brought them into the temple of the Lord and the high priest said, "Cast lots to see who will spin the gold, the amianthus, the linen, the silk, the hyacinth blue, the scarlet and the pure purple." The pure purple and scarlet fell by lot to Mary. And she, taking them, went to her house. At that time, Zechariah became mute and Simeon [originally Samuel, but here replaced with an ancient Syriac gloss] took his place until Zechariah was able to speak again. And Mary took the scarlet and began to spin.

Commentary

10.1.a. The council of priests have decided it is time to weave a new veil for the temple. The high priest asked for the undefiled virgins of the tribe of David to be called. A search revealed that there were seven virgins available for the task. The virgins of the 'tribe of David' in the temple were called because the veil that had to be created was the most precious veil in the temple and it was work that would have been the most highly esteemed.

Hock, 1995, 51, fn. 10:2, observed that 'there was no tribe of David'. It is more likely that the term had not been encountered before. The unconventional reference may refer to the house of David reckoned through matrilineal descent. Arguments can be derived from a number of items in the Protevangelium and the Old Testament.

There is a legitimate distaste for the tribe of Reuben in (1.2) and (6.3) and underneath it lurks the notion of how Joseph replaced Reuben in the birthright. The process involved Rachel as a matriarch in which her son Joseph is matrilineally descended from her. In turn, through Joseph, one of his descendants was David. Rachel is his matriarch. Similarly, Anna also appears to view Rachel as her matriarch. In addition, through other descendants of David , also recognized through matrilineal descent, there is a 'tribe' based on matrilineal descent from David. It is through this 'tribe' that the Messiah would be born. They are of the house of David and would be able to bear the Messiah (not through paternal descent but through matrilineal descent).

This may have arisen because in the years following the Babylonian exile the paternal descent of David seems to have disappeared. Zerubbabel is a paternal descendant of a king in the line of David, But Jeremiah 22:18–19, 24, prophesied that no descendant of this king would ever be king again. Nevertheless, Jeremiah looked ahead to a future king.

> Antiphon. The days are surely coming, says the Lord, when I will raise up for David a righteous Branch, and he shall reign as king and deal wisely, and shall execute justice and righteousness in the land. In his days Judah will be saved and Israel will live in safety. And this is the name by which he will be called" 'The Lord is our righteousness.' (Jeremiah 23:5–6).

> Antiphon. A shoot shall come out from the stock of Jesse, and a branch shall grow out of his roots. The spirit of the Lord shall rest on him, the spirit of wisdom and understanding, the spirit of counsel and might, the spirit of knowledge and the fear of the Lord. (Isaiah 11:1–2).

> Antiphon. The Lord says to my lord, 'Sit at my right hand until I make your enemies your footstool.' The Lord sends out from Zion your mighty sceptre. Rule in the midst of your foes. (Psalm 110:1–2).

If the paternal line has disappeared, it does not mean that descendants of David are not known through matrilineal descent and the priests appear to have adopted this as a route towards the Messiah. This is suggested by several items in the Protevangelium which all focus on the question of the Messiah. In the messianic song of Anna, (6.3), the high priests gave a messianic blessing to Mary in (6.2). Also, in Anna's song, (6.3), she compares herself with Rachel who had previously not given birth, until the Lord opened her womb, and she bore Joseph. It is through matrilineal descent through Joseph that David was born, and Rachel is the matriarch of David. Anna appears to identify with Rachel as her matriarch and in matrilineal descent she may be a descendant of David as suggested in (2.2). This may account for her evident belittlement of the tribe of Reuben documented in (1.2) and (6.3). Mary is also credited in the blessings of (7.2) with the concept that the Messiah will come through her. Thus, Mary is already implicated in the matrilineal line of decent from the house of David. Now, Mary is confirmed by the high priest as being of 'the tribe of David' and it is through matrilineal descent that she is of the house of David. Similarly, there are seven, possibly a ritual number, of other undefiled virgins of the tribe of David. It appears that the temple is keeping in contact with girls who are descendants of David through matrilineal descent because one of them might be a potential mother of the Messiah. They likely all received the traditional ritual blessing of the priests that Mary received in (6.2). Mary is not the only such girl that the temple is interested in. Nevertheless, given what has happened in (7.2) and (7.3), the priests have decided that Mary is the chosen one.

10.1.b. The idea of having women weaving the veils for the tabernacle had been the case in ancient Israel.

> Antiphon. All the skillful women spun with their hands, and brought what they had spun in blue and purple and crimson yarns and fine linen; all the women whose hearts moved them to use their skill spun the goats' hair. (Exodus 35:25–26).

Antiphon. All those with skill among the workers made the tabernacle with ten curtains; they were made of fine twisted linen, and blue, purple, and crimson yarns, with cherubim skillfully worked into them. (Exodus 36:8).

One would also expect that it would be the case at the time of the Protevangelium. The following explorations exhibit evidence that this was indeed the case.

10.1.c. Dalia Marx provides much evidence that weaving and spinning were regarded as traditional female tasks from biblical and rabbinical sources.[33] She notes that in what is essentially a medical manual there are descriptions of everyday activities that are clearly divided between those typical for men and others typical for women.

Antiphon. After what fashion is the inspection of skin blemishes? The man is inspected like one who hoes, and like one that gathers olives. The woman like one who rolls out dough, and like one who breastfeeds her child, and like [a woman] who weaves at an upright loom, [if the sign is] beneath the right armpit. Rabbi Yehudah says: Also like [a woman] who spins flax [if the sign is] beneath the left [armpit]. (Mishnah Negaim 2.4).

She also observes that textile crafts are mentioned as female activities in the book of Proverbs. A capable wife is said to have a variety of specific qualities.

Antiphon. She seeks wool and flax, and works with willing hands. (Proverbs 31:13).

Antiphon. She puts her hands to the distaff, and her hands hold the spindle. (Proverbs 31:19).

Additionally, she notes that males are clearly discouraged or demeaned if they engage in these types of activities.

Antiphon. May the guilt fall on the head of Joab, and on all his father's house; and may the house of Joab never be without one who has a discharge, or who is leprous, or who holds a spindle, or who falls by the sword, or who lacks food!" (2 Samuel 3:29).

Later recollections of the rabbis and other early writings also provide insight into the fact that young virginal women were involved in the manufacture of textiles for the Second Temple. Much of this has been discussed before but for the purpose of this volume it is useful to summarize it.

Amann, 1910:218 had cited the Talmud to discount the theory of young girls weaving in the temple but it was not properly referenced. Later, however, it was certain that he was referring to Mishnah Shekalim 8:5. Some twenty-four years after Amann's commentary, J. N. Epstein published a seminal paper in 1934 challenging our understanding of this mishnah.[34] He claimed that whereas the text reads "it was made of 820,000" (that is, 82 myriads) it should read "The veil of the Temple] was made by eighty-two young girls." The latter phrase

---

[33] Dalia Marx, *Tractates Tamid, Middot and Qinnim: A Feminist Commentary* (Mohr Siebeck, Tübingen, Germany, 2013), 38–39.
[34] J. N. Epstein, "Some Variae Lectiones in the Yerushalmi I: The Leiden MS" (*Tarbiz* 5, 1933–34), 261.

is a *baraita* [that is, a tradition in the Jewish oral law not incorporated in the Mishnah] and indicates that the mishnah was rewritten at some point.[35] The form with "young girls" is quoted twice in the Babylonian Talmud (*B. Hullin* 90b and *B. Tamid* 29b). Rashi's commentary on B. Hullin 90b and Pseudo-Rashi's commentary *on B. Tamid* 29b refer to maidens as present in the text in front of them and following them; modern scholars do likewise.

Ilan,1997:142, reconstructed the convoluted historical redaction of Mishnah Shekalim 8.5 in the following words.

When the Mishnah was redacted, for various reasons the women weavers were edited out. However, since a certain tradition, not included in the Mishnah originally, did mention eighty-two female weavers, this part of the tradition, preserved as a *baraita*, was at a later date reincorporated into the mishnaic text. At a final stage, another copyist, who misunderstood the tradition, altered the reading, so that the women were again censored out of the text.

Frédéric Manns also argued that Mishnah Shekalim 8:5 did indeed refer to the number of girls who worked on the curtain.[36] Noting that they are called "young girls" rather than "virgins", he proposed that the weavers had to be prepubescent. He compared this with the masculine form found in Mishnah Tamid 1.1 for the young priests who kept watch in the temple at night.

The overseer of the weavers is also mentioned among the *memunin* – the overseers of the temple – in Mishnah Shekalim 5:1.

In some extra-rabbinical sources, it is stressed that the veil of the temple was woven by virgins. Marx, 2013, 41, observed that Pseudo-Rashi on the gemara for Tamid maintains that they were young girls who had not yet seen menstrual blood. He asserts that this was a precaution taken to ensure that they did not cause impurity to the veil, although this sensitivity is not found in the classical rabbinic literature." (Marx, 2013, 41).

She also observed that according to Pseudo-Rashi, in spite of the precautions, the weaving of the veil also involved a certain risk – one of the weaving girls may begin to menstruate for the first time without noticing, causing the veil to become impure. And although not specified in classical rabbinic texts, according to Pseudo-Rashi, this is why it had to be immersed.

There are additional references to women who wove the temple curtains in other rabbinical sources.

> Antiphon. R. Nahman said: Rab stated that the women who wove the [Temple] curtains received their wages from the Temple funds but I maintain [that they received them] from the sums consecrated for Temple repairs, since the curtains were a substitute for builder's work.

---

[35] Tal Ilan, *Mine & Yours are Hers, Retrieving Women's History from Rabbinic Literature* (Brill: Leiden, 1997), 142; Saul Lieberman, *Hellenism in Jewish Palestine*, New York, 1950, 167.
[36] Frédéric Manns, *Essais sur le judéo-christianisme* (Jerusalem: Franciscan Printing Press, 1997, 105–109.

An objection was raised: The women who wove the [Temple] curtains, and the house of Garmo [who were in charge] of the preparation of the showbread, and the house of Abtinas [who were in charge] of the preparation of the incense, received their wages from the Temple funds! – There [it may be replied] the reference is [to the curtains] of the gates; for R. Zera related in the name of Rab: There were thirteen curtains in the Second Temple, seven corresponding to the seven gates, one for the entrance to the Hekal, one for the entrance to the 'Ulam, two [at the entrance] to the Debir and two [above them and] corresponding to them in the upper storey. (B. Kethuboth, Folio 106a).

It is also believed that within the temple precincts there was a Chamber of the Curtain wherein women worked to create the curtains (Mishnah Middot 1:1).

The *Pesikta Rabbati* is a Jewish midrash containing discourses for feasts, fasts, and special sabbaths. Many scholars have assumed that it was compiled in Europe sometime after 845.[37] On the other hand, W. G. Braude, 1968, who published the work noted that M. Friedmann, who published a critical edition of the work in 1880, argued that it was composed in 355. Braude found this suggestion attractive because it was supported by internal evidence. The Amoraim cited in the *Pesikta Rabbati* lived in Palestine in the third and fourth centuries. Braude concluded that the most likely date for the *Pesikta Rabbati's* redaction is the seventh century, although the sixth century is also a possibility. However, he also concluded that "it is certain that the greatest part of the material in the text goes back to Talmudic times," that is, to the third and fourth centuries.

Of special interest is the account in the *Peskita Rabbati* (Piska 26) of the destruction of Jerusalem and the First Temple by Nebuchadnezzar. The enemies came and set up a platform on the Temple Mount where they sat and planned the burning of the temple. The homily continues with the following dire account.

Antiphon. As they were deliberating, they lifted their eyes and saw four angels descending, in their hands four flaming torches which they placed at the four corners of the Temple, setting it on fire. When the High Priest saw that the Temple was on fire, he took the keys and cast them heavenward. He opened his mouth and cried out: "Here are the keys of Thy House; I have been an unworthy custodian of it." He started to go, but the enemies seized him and slaughtered him at the altar in the very place where he used to offer the daily sacrifice. His daughter ran out wildly, crying: "Woe unto me! My father, the delight of my eyes!" They seized her and slaughtered her also and mingled her blood with the blood of her father.

When the priests and Levites saw that the Temple was on fire, they took their harps and trumpets and let themselves fall with them into the flames and were consumed. When the virgins who wove the curtain for the Sanctuary saw that the Temple was on fire, they let themselves fall into the flames, so that the enemies should not violate them, and were consumed. (Pesikta Rabbati, Piska 26, after Braude, 1968:535).

Another interesting reference to the virgin weavers is found in 2 Baruch, dated c. 95–129 CE, written not long after the destruction of the temple in 70. The lamentation opens with a description of the destruction of Jerusalem by the Babylonians in 587 BCE. Given the date it was written, however, scholars believe that although

[37] Pesikta Rabbati (*Discourses for Feasts, Fasts, and Special Sabbaths*), translated by W. G. Braude (New Haven and London: Yale University Press, 1968), 2, 21.

the destruction is ascribed to the Babylonians, the destruction in fact relates to the fall of Jerusalem under the Romans. Baruch, who depicts himself as sitting in front of the doors of the temple, laments.

> Antiphon. You, priests, take the keys of the sanctuary, and cast them to the highest heaven, and give them to the Lord and say, "Guard your house yourself, because, behold, we have been found to be false stewards."
>
> And you, virgins who spin fine linen, and silk with gold of Ophir, make haste and take all things, and cast them into the fire, so that it may carry them to him who made them. And the flame sends them to him who created them, so that the enemies do not take possession of them. (2 Baruch 10:18–19).

A passage in 2 Maccabees discusses the intrusion of Heliodorus, under instructions from the king, Seleucus IV Philopator (187–175 BCE), into the temple precincts to retrieve the wealth of the temple. The description of the ensuing commotion is of interest.

> Antiphon. To see the appearance of the high priest was to be wounded at heart, for his face and the change in his color disclosed the anguish of his soul. For terror and bodily trembling had come over the man, which plainly showed to those who looked at him the pain lodged in his heart. People also hurried out of their houses in crowds to make a general supplication because the holy place was about to be brought into dishonor. Women, girded with sackcloth under their breasts, thronged the streets.
>
> Some of the young women who were kept indoors ran together to the gates, and some to the walls, while others peered out of the windows. And holding up their hands to heaven, they all made supplication. (2 Maccabees 3:16–20).

It is likely that 'the young women who were kept indoors' (NRSV), 'the girls secluded indoors' (NJB), and 'the virgins that were kept in' (Septuagint), according to the respective translations, are the same as the group of virgin weavers that are discussed in the Protevangelium.

10.1.d. With the arrival of seven undefiled virgins of the tribe of David, the high priest [Simeon] suddenly remembered the child Mary who was of the tribe of David and undefiled. She was no longer in the temple and had recently been assigned to Joseph as her ward. He ordered the officers to go and fetch her and they did so.

This is an unusual procedure and suggests that the high priest may have been aroused by the Lord to call Mary to the meeting.

The naming of Mary as being of the tribe of David is significant. It is the first and only time that such a clear designation has been made. Yes, there have been many strong inferences and Mary has been directly implicated in the messianic story. Yet, it is also a part of her story knowing that the priests of the temple are interested in young girls of the house of David and would like to keep track of them. It is also a part of Mary's story that she is not the only undefiled virgin of the house of David in the temple. It also shows that she recently left the temple – since she is still referred to as 'the child Mary' in (6.1) – for otherwise it would be too risky to have her back. Now that Mary has left the temple precincts and is under the protection of Joseph she is no longer with the other undefiled daughters of the Hebrews. Implicitly, this indicates that there are common quarters for them as has been suggested in some of the previous examples in (10.1b). They had lived in an enclosed and segregated area until they had reached the age of 12. In the normal course, then they would have had marriages arranged for them. And the priests would have a special interest in their offspring so as to keep track of the house of David.

This is an important development for the high priest [Simeon] has clarified that Mary is of the tribe of David in front of a group of seven undefiled virgins of the tribe of David.

10.2.a. The young virgins were brought to the temple and the high priest asked them to cast lots to see who would spin the various products that were needed for the veil. These are named as gold, amianthus, linen, silk, the hyacinth-blue, the scarlet and the pure purple. Among them, four are listed in Exodus 35:25 (or Exodus 36:8): hyacinth-blue, pure purple (a red purple much more precious than the preceding shade), scarlet, and byssus (a very fine linen from India).

These materials are what are required for the veil that protects the Holy of Holies as suggested by Hock, 1995: 51, fn. 10:2.

> Antiphon. You shall make a curtain of blue, purple, and crimson yarns, and of fine twisted linen; it shall be made with cherubim skillfully worked into it. You shall hang it on four pillars of acacia overlaid with gold, which have hooks of gold and rest on four bases of silver. You shall hang the curtain under the clasps, and bring the ark of the covenant inside within the curtain; and the curtain shall separate for you the holy place from the most holy. You shall put the mercy seat on the ark of the covenant in the most holy place. (Exodus 26:31–34).

The curtain separates the Holy of Holies from the sanctuary (the Holy Place). This same division between the Holy Place and the Holy of Holies existed in Solomon's Temple (1 Kings 6:16) and in Herod's Temple (Exodus 26:34, fn. e, NJB). Although , it must be remembered that the contents in the Second Temple did not include the ark of the covenant. Rather, it had a substitute consisting of a mercy-seat with a cover (Heb. *kapporet*) over the mercy-seat with cherubim attached upon it. The term *kapporet* is from the root *kaphar*, 'to cover', but also 'to perform the expiation', 'to obliterate'. The *kapporet* is presented in Exodus 25:17 and Exodus 35:12 as being distinct from the ark.[38]

After casting lots, the pure purple and scarlet fell to Mary. This is a divine intervention assigning Mary to these materials. It is another phenomenon that is unusual. In the present case, it suggests that Mary and the other weavers are preparing the *kapporet* on the mercy seat. This is a different situation than weaving a veil of the temple, or the curtain separating the Holy of Holies from the Holy Place. It is a task for weaving the cover of the

---

[38] Exodus 25:7, fn. h. NJB. Accepted translation of the word *kapporet*, from the root *kaphar*, 'to cover', but also 'to perform the expiation', 'to obliterate'. The *kapporet* is presented here and at 35:12 as being distinct from the ark. It figures without the ark, in the post-exilic ritual for the Day of Expiation, Lv 16:15; and 1 Ch 28:11 calls the Holy of Holies the 'hall of the mercy-seat'. It seems that the mercy-seat and the winged creatures attached to it in the post-exilic Temple, were substituted for the ark and winged creatures of Solomon's Temple. The Priestly description has put them both together, *see* v. 21. Yahweh appears on the mercy-seat, and this is where he speaks to Moses, v. 22; Lv 16:2; Nb 7:89.

mercy-seat in the Holy of Holies and it is the holiest item in the temple. It marks the location which in ancient times marked the place where the Lord would theoretically be seated and address the Israelites.

Hock, 1995, 51, fn. 10:2, suggests that 80 women are required to weave a temple veil. This may be the case, from the previous information on temple veils that covered a doorway, but in the present case – after the Babylonian exile – 8 girls would be able to weave the *kapporet* and attach the cherubim to it as the cover of the mercy-seat. This is not an immense curtain veil, and 8 girls would be sufficient for it.

This addresses any concerns about the massive size of the veils and curtains in the temple that have been reported. The weaving of the cover of the mercy-seat changes the scale completely and it would not be unusual to have a group of eight trained weavers working on it. The *kapporet* of woven purple and attached cherubim is of royal dignity and in ancient times would shelter the 'seat of the Lord'.

10.2.b. In these situations, Mary had little choice in anything she did. It is the priests (with help from God, through the casting of lots) who are running things. Their role is important in the story of Mary for they are hoping that she may be the mother of the Messiah as indicated by the blessings that they have given her in (6.2) and in permitting the 'undefiled daughters of the Hebrews' to assist Anna in (6,1). In addition, when the temple welcomed Mary into the temple, she was directly implicated in the messianic age in the blessing of (7.2) and in the remarkable events in (7.3) and (7.4). In (8.1) Mary had an elevated position in the temple because she is like a dove that dwelt there and is under the protection of God, for she is described as receiving food from the hand of an angel. And in (10.1), the high priest was inspired to invite Mary back to the council for the veil to participate, not alone but with seven other undefiled virgins of the tribe of David and to declare in front of them and the priests that Mary herself was of the tribe of David. This declaration with witnesses from both the tribe of David and the priests is not to be taken lightly.

Given that the 'tribe of David' reckons matrilineal descent from David and that her daughter Mary is of the tribe of David then Anna herself was at one time an 'undefiled virgin of the tribe of David'. This fits in with numerous indications in the Protevangelium.

Anna was described as a person 'who feared the Lord', whose 'parents were righteous', and who had been 'trained according to the law of Moses' (1.1.a). This was suggested because these were characteristics of the wife of Joachim's namesake (1.1.a), however, in the early sections of the Protevangelium, Anna demonstrated that these were also her own characteristics, and she likely became that person by being 'an undefiled virgin of the tribe of David' in the temple.

It accounts for the incident in which Anna's handmaid Judith offered her a headband' that had 'a royal appearance' in (2.2).

It accounts for Anna's proclamation that her soul had 'been magnified' the day that Mary was born (5.2) since now Mary herself was a possible candidate for being the mother of the Messiah.

It accounts for the blessings that Mary received when the priests and the high priests came to visit her when she was one year old. It was likely that Anna herself had received the same ritual blessing of the priests that had been given to Mary (6.2) if she had resided in the temple as 'an undefiled virgin of the tribe of David'.

It accounts for the matrilineal suggestions of Anna in her messianic song in (6.3) that hinted at Rachel being her matriarch and emphasized the fact that Rachel was a matriarch of David. Knowing that Anna is of the tribe of David, necessarily means that as a descendent of David , Rachel is her matriarch. Also, knowing that Anna is of the tribe of David, would symbolize her antagonism to Reuben at the time of Joachim's offering in (1.2) and her insult to the 'sons of Reuben' in her song in (6.3).

All of these items in the Protevangelium take on a new appearance once it is recognized that they are not random incidents but are associated with Anna who is a descendent of David through a matrilineal association that goes back to the time of Rachel.

The story of Mary is not only about Mary, but it is also about Anna (note the disproportionate attention given to Anna rather than to Joachim in the narrative) and about a group of priests in the temple who help her and guide her in her vocation. The priests, or at least a subset of priests, are not in the background but are active supporters of Mary. They are another voice, and they too speak to the reader about Mary. Given what has happened with the messianic prophecies in (6.2) (from the high priest) and (6.3) (Anna's messianic song) and also the startling prophesies in (7.3) and (7.4) there are messianic insights into Mary that justify that her conception be marked by a prophecy, following (4.4.b), from Isaiah 65:17–18). It is through the conception of Mary that God is beginning the creation of 'new heavens and a new earth' and it is time to rejoice for ever in what is happening. He is about to create Jerusalem as a joy, and its people as a delight'. This was the key moment in foretelling the messianic age that was about to begin.

10.2.c. We have met the high priest Zechariah in (8.3) and now hear that he has suddenly gone mute, and 'Samuel' has taken his place until he is able to speak again. In a later note in (24.4), Amann observes that 'Simeon' has been chosen by lot to replace Zechariah who had been murdered in the sanctuary of the temple. He then refers to the Syriac version of (10.2) which includes the ancient gloss of 'Simeon' in reference to 'Samuel' as recorded here. Amann agrees that Samuel should certainly be read as Simeon.

10.2.d. And Mary, taking the purple and the scarlet, went to her house. This is unusual because Mary is no longer with the other undefiled virgins and leaves the temple to weave at home. She took the scarlet and began to spin.

The Annunciation (Mary)

11.1   And she took the pitcher and went out to draw water, and behold, a voice said, "Hail, you who have received grace, the Lord is with you; blessed are you among women." And she looked around, to the right and to the left, to see where this voice came from. And, trembling, she returned to her house and put down the pitcher. And taking the purple, she sat down on her seat and drew it out.

11.2   And behold, an angel of the Lord stood before her, saying, "Do not fear, Mary; for you have found grace before the Lord of all and you shall conceive according to his word." Upon hearing this, she examined it, saying, "Shall I conceive by the Lord, the living God? And shall I bring forth as every woman brings forth?"

11.3   And the angel of the Lord said, "Not so, Mary; for the power of the Lord shall overshadow you; wherefore also the Holy One to be born of you shall be called the Son of the Most High. And you shall call his name Jesus; for he shall save his people from their sins." And Mary said, "Behold, the servant of the Lord – in his presence; be it [done] to me, according to your word."

Commentary

11.1.a. The scene of the annunciation to Mary shows her going about her normal tasks. The story begins with the action of Mary taking a pitcher and going out to draw water. In biblical translations, one generally draws water from a "well' or a "spring" and that is the case here. Meeting the bride at the well is a common motif in Hebrew love stories.

It is likely that the story of Rebekah influences the present scene. Abraham, seeking a spouse for his son Isaac, sent an emissary to his homeland to find a suitable wife for him. The emissary met Rebekah – with a pitcher on her shoulder – at a well (Genesis 24:11–61). Later, Isaac met Rebekah and takes her as his wife (Genesis 24:62–67). Similarly, Jacob met Rachel at a well (Genesis 29:1–14). After much travail (fourteen years of toil for his uncle) he married Rachel. Also, Moses met his first wife at a well (Exodus 2:16–22).

> Antiphon. Before he had finished speaking, there was Rebekah, who was born to Bethuel son of Milcah, the wife of Nahor, Abraham's brother, coming out with her water jar on her shoulder. The girl was very fair to look upon, a virgin whom no man had known. She went down to the spring, filled her jar, and came up. (Genesis 24:15–16).

11.1.b. Mary, as she approached the well, suddenly heard a voice say, "Hail, you who have received grace, the Lord is with you; blessed are you among women."

The first phrase is a salutation to Mary and names her as one who had received God's grace. This recalls the moment in (7.4) when Mary was three years old and had entered the temple and 'the Lord God sent his grace upon her.' Now, at 12 years of age, Mary is being hailed with a mention of that grace, apparently a permanent gift of God. Mary essentially received the grace at the end of her infancy, after she had been weaned and brought to the temple. The nature of that grace is going to be revealed in the second phrase of the salutation.

In this phrase, 'the Lord is with you' corresponds to 'the presence of the Lord is with you.' It describes a spiritual state of Mary who lives in the presence of the Lord during her earthly life. The Protevangelium has its own way of describing this state. In (8.1) it is said that 'Mary was in the temple of the Lord as if she were a dove that dwelt there, and she received food from the hand of an angel'. On other occasions, it is said that 'Mary is raised in the [heavenly] holy of holies and received food from the hand of an angel' (13.2) and (15.3).

The third phrase declares that Mary is 'blessed among women'. This is the first time that the expression has been used. The title has a specific meaning because it indicates that Mary will be the mother of the Messiah. It has not happened yet, but the process is about to begin. The event is intended to happen because, from the moment of her conception, a nazirite vow had been placed on Mary through her mother and she would be holy to God all the days of her life. The time has now arrived for Mary to freely accept the vow and confirm that she is the 'servant of the Lord' for all the days of her life.

11.1.c. The voice that Mary heard – a voice that she could not locate – had a significant effect on her. It was the 'Voice of God' (Heb. *bat kol*, lit. 'daughter voice').[39] When Mary heard the voice, she looked around and could not find where it was coming from, and, trembling, went home. *The bat kol* could be heard by any individual or group regardless of their connection with God.

> Antiphon. All these things my hand has made, and so all these things are mine, says the Lord. But this is the one to whom I will look, to the humble and contrite in spirit, who trembles at my word. (Isaiah 66:2).

> Antiphon. Listen, an uproar from the city! A voice from the temple! The voice of the Lord, dealing retribution to his enemies! (Isaiah 66:6).

The Voice of God is Mary's suitor. It praises Mary publicly, in a voice that anyone could hear. It has been noted that 'unclean spirits' (Zechariah 13:1–2) would hear the Voice of God as there is no restriction on who hears it. It has been noted in (10.2.b) that the priests were very interested in Mary and would hear the voice in the temple and they likely had watchers on Mary who was doing spinning for the cover of the mercy-seat. The priests are aware of what is happening.

---

[39] Zervos, 2019, 41. The existence of the almost personified, hypostasized Voice of God is widely attested in the Hebrew Scriptures and occurs throughout the literature of the late and post-second temple periods in the pseudepigrapha, targums, and the Hellenistic Jewish and rabbinical writings.

Previously, Mary had been spinning the scarlet, (10.2), but there is no indication in the narrative that the former scene is closely related in time to the present episode. There is nothing in the text to suggest that Mary suddenly changed from scarlet to purple. She may very well have completed spinning the scarlet and was naturally moving onwards to the purple.

Nevertheless, there are narrative reasons for Mary spinning the purple at this point, not because it is the most expensive as several Greek commentators have suggested (Amann, 1910, 216) but because it is intended as a cover for the mercy-seat, the most sacred object in the Holy of Holies.

11.2.a. Suddenly, an angel of the Lord stood before her. The angel first asked her not to fear. There is nothing in the narrative to imply that Mary encountered angels as a regular fact of her daily life. This may be the first angel that she has encountered and her reaction, as is common in the scriptures, may have been fear. The angel said that she had 'found grace before the Lord of all' and that she would 'conceive according to his word'. The first phrase is important and is similar to the phrases in (7.4) and (11.1). This is the third time that Mary has been said to have 'found grace before the Lord'. The triple repetition of this phrase and the repetition of its Protevangelium equivalent – 'being raised in the [heavenly] holy of holies and being fed by the hand of an angel' indicate that this is a permanent status of Mary.

Amann, 1910:223, is not happy with the phrase 'you shall conceive according to his word' and considers it vague. It appears to him that it suggests that Mary conceived after hearing the words of the angel. In fact, as he points out in his commentary, some later revisions of the Protevangelium took it very literally and argued that 'Mary conceived in her ear'. The phrase 'according to his word' may however, have been suggested by Isaiah's description of God's word, a word that always accomplishes its purpose.

> (Antiphon). For as the rain and the snow come down from heaven, and do not return there until they have watered the earth, making it bring forth and sprout, giving seed to the sower and bread to the eater, so shall my word be that goes out from my mouth; it shall not return to me empty, but it shall accomplish that which I purpose, and succeed in the thing for which I sent it. (Isaiah 55:10–11).

When Mary heard this, she examined it and asked two questions. The first concerns the possibility of conceiving by a divine action and the second concerns bringing forth as every woman brings forth. In a spiritual sense, Mary lives in the holy of holies in the heavenly temple, but in a material sense, she lives out her life on earth. To all appearances she is a pious Jewish girl of exceptional holiness.

Anna's vow has consecrated her as holy to the Lord all the days of her life, but Mary has not had much say about it. This lack of personal freedom for a young girl would not have been unusual in the culture in which she lived. It is only now, when God comes calling, that she will have to make some real personal decisions. The entire question of childbirth is of concern to the Protevangelium because it is related to Mary's ritual purity. One can see this in the narrative because Mary herself shows an anxiety about becoming pregnant and also about giving birth. Her unease is related to the question of ritual purity and not virginity.

11.2.b. To better understand Mary's reaction to her situation it is necessary to look into the concept of female purity that was an integral part of her upbringing. For this purpose, some selections from a study by Tirzah Meacham (leBeit Yoreh) on female purity and *niddah* need to be considered.[40]

1. Menstrual impurity must be seen in the context of the biblical purity system. The purity system of the Bible chiefly involved the temple, sacrifices and priestly gifts, all of which had to be guarded from ritual impurity. The penalty for polluting the Temple is *karet*, excision from the people of Israel or a divine decree of death. The Land had to be guarded from moral impurity lest the people of Israel be vomited out of the land as their predecessors had been.

2. Chapter 15 of Leviticus serves as the basis for the Jewish menstrual laws. The Hebrew term used for menstruation in Leviticus 15:19, 20, 24, and 33 is *niddatah*, which has as its root *ndh*, a word meaning "separation," usually as a result of impurity.

3. [The root reflects] the physical separation of women during menstruation (or abnormal uterine bleeding or the seven or fourteen days immediately postpartum) from physical contact or from certain activities in which they would normally engage at other times.

4. In other parts of the Bible, the term *niddah* was transferred to include abominable acts, objects (Ezekiel 7:19–20) or status, especially sexual sins (Leviticus 20:21) and idolatry. The use of the term *niddah* to describe the impurity of the land due to sin is found in Lamentations 1:8 and Ezra 9:11 and as an antonym of holiness in 2 Chronicles 29:5. These usages of the term may have influenced subsequent reactions to the state of menstruation. The term *niddah* was transformed into a metaphorical expression for sin and impurity in general.

5. It must be emphasized that being in a state of ritual impurity was not in itself sinful because menstruation [is a] part of normal physiology. The sin mentioned in Leviticus 15:31 is the act of polluting of God's cultic space by one's presence while ritually impure.

6. When a woman begins to have contractions and sees blood prior to a birth, she becomes *niddah*. All the restrictions in reference to contact with a *niddah* apply until she gives birth, at which time the birth regulations apply. This has had a major impact on the level of contact a laboring woman can have with her spouse and whether fathers are allowed in delivery rooms. Blood which is connected to labor contractions retains the status of *niddah* blood unless the contractions cease.

Tirzah Meacham (leBeit Yoreh), "Female Purity (Niddah)"

If we insert ourselves into the narrative, it is clear that because of her years of service to God in the temple, the laws of ritual purity and temple holiness would be second nature to Mary. But what does the angel's message mean for someone who has been welcomed into the heavenly holy of holies? How could she conceive according

---

[40] Tirzah Meacham (leBeit Yoreh), "Female Purity (Niddah)," in *Jewish Women: A Comprehensive Historical Encyclopedia* (Jewish Women's Archive, 2009).

to God's word when she becomes niddah? How could she give birth to the child without defiling God's holy work when she becomes niddah? In either case she would be contaminating the cultic space of God. It is small wonder that upon hearing this, she examined it. Indeed, this is the law of holiness under which Mary lived.

> Antiphon. Shall I open the womb and not deliver? says the Lord; shall I the one who delivers, shut the womb? says your God. (Isaiah 66:9).

11.3.a. The answer of the angel remains vague. It does not reply directly to the questions posed by Mary. To say that 'the power of the Lord shall overshadow you' is mysterious and it remains to see how it relates to the idea of preservation from defilement. Mary had asked two questions, but the angel replied with a single answer. Mary, however, trusts the Lord and is reassured by it. She then affirms the vow that her mother had made for her so long ago,

Mary said, 'Behold, the servant of the Lord – in his presence; be it [done] to me according to your word'. The inclusion of the phrase 'in his presence' demonstrates that Mary is speaking direcrtly to the Lord.

11.3.b. This chapter marks a significant change in the narrative since Mary speaks for the first time. Until now she has been a real presence but a subdued one. There have been few expressions of her individuality, precocious walking at the age of six months (6.1) and dancing on the third step of the altar in the heavenly temple (7.3). Until now, Mary has been portrayed as a character that is not in charge of her own life. It was Anna who imposed a nazirite vow on her (4.1) and who confined her to a home sanctuary (6.1). It was Anna and Joachim who brought her to the temple of the Lord (7.2). It was God who sent his grace upon her (7.3).

It was the priests, after consulting with God, who decided what to do with Mary at the age of twelve (8.3). It was the priests who gave her to Joseph who would act as her ward (9.1). It was Joseph who left Mary in his house (9.3). It was the officers of the temple who brought Mary back to the temple to be selected for work on a temple veil (10.1). And now God has selected Mary for a special purpose – to bear the 'Holy One who shall be called the Son of the Most High' and who 'shall save his people from their sins' (11.1). And Mary speaks

Yet, these stories tell us something about Mary. She is a female child living at a time when girls had no independence; lives were severely constrained on all sides. As a girl, her submissive behavior would be well accepted and approved in the culture to which she belonged. Moreover, Mary is obedient – to her parents, to the priests, to Joseph, and to God.

At the age of twelve, or shortly thereafter, Mary has a voice and speaks for the first time – expressing her concerns about what the angel has told her (11.2). And, in her newly found "adulthood" she is ready to take personal responsibility. She consents to the vow imposed on her so long ago by Anna (4.1). She affirms that she is 'the servant of the Lord – in his presence'. She willingly undertakes the mysterious vocation that God asks of her (11.3) and replies 'be it (done) to me, according to your word'.

11.3.c. It remains to take a closer look at the angelic annunciation to Mary: "Not so, Mary; for the power of the Lord shall overshadow you; wherefore also the Holy One to be born of you shall be called the Son of the Most High. And you shall call his name Jesus; for he shall save his people from their sins."

the power of the Lord shall overshadow you

A more precise meaning of this phrase is not discussed here. A detailed visual portrayal of this event, will be described in (19.2). The description of the event is delayed but the effects of it take place shortly after Mary gives her consent. The consequences will be discussed in (12.1) and (12.2).

the Holy One to be born of you

The expression 'Holy One' refers to the unique God of Israel. Of the 8 uses of Holy One in the Old Testament, four of them are in Isaiah, but they all have the same meaning. One of the favourite titles of Isaiah for the Lord is 'Holy One of Israel'. Of 29 uses of 'Holy One of Israel' in the Old Testament, 24 of them are in Isaiah. Thus, the use of Holy One in the pronouncement of the angel of annunication shows Isaian influence and it is directed to a messianic age in which Mary has received a blessing that 'in the last days, the Lord will manifest his redemption to the children of Israel' through her (7.3).

The angel is speaking to Mary and the phrase indicates that the Holy One is to be born of Mary. The usage indicates that the Holy One refers to the child of Mary, who is named Jesus' as the angel instructed. Thus, Jesus is the Holy One and has divine status. Jesus is also the biological son of Mary and has human status.

shall be called the Son of the Most High

In Psalm 110, a messianic psalm, 'of David', opens with the unusual statement: 'Yahweh declared to my Lord, 'Take your seat at my right hand, till I have made your enemies your footstool' (Psalm 110:1, NJB). The opening phrase depicts David addressing Yahweh about the Messiah, a future descendant of his, and he refers to him as 'Lord'. Therefore, David looking into the future addresses one of his descendants with the standard divine title, 'Lord'. This indicates that the Messiah, a 'son of David', is more than human for he shares the divine name. The psalm continues with the statement: 'Yahweh has sworn an oath he will never retract, you are a priest for ever of the order of Melchizedek. (Psalm 110:4, NJB). This indicates that the Messiah has an eternal inheritance as a 'a priest for ever', and this is an oath of Yahweh that 'he will never retract'.

The reference to Melchizedek in the psalm directs the reader to an early text in Genesis 14:17–24 which discusses a meeting of Abram[41] with Melchizedek, king of Salem (the subsequent Jewish tradition identifies Salem with Jerusalem, Psalm 76:2). Melchizedek as well as being king of Salem is a 'priest of God Most High'. During the meeting, Abram bestows a blessing to the king of Sodom in which he swears 'to the Lord, God most High, maker of heaven and earth (Genesis 14:22). In this blessing, in this context, Abram is identifying 'the Lord' with 'God Most High, maker of heaven and earth'.

---

[41] Abram is later renamed 'Abraham' at the time when Yahweh made a covenant with him, Genesis 17:1–8.

The concepts that are being considered here, stretch over centuries. Briefly, one is considering a series of parallels:

> Melchizedek is king of Salem and priest of God Most High
> David is king of Jerusalem and priest of the Lord
> Messiah is king of Jerusalem and priest for ever of the order of Melchizedek

The prerogatives of the Messiah, worldwide sovereignty and perpetual priesthood are no more conferred by earthly vestiture than were those of the mysterious Melchizedek.

The annunciation text then says that the son of Mary should be called the 'Son of the Most High'.

> *you shall call his name Jesus; for he shall save his people from their sins*

The phrasing here uses a Semitic form by saying 'call his name Jesus' as opposed to the previous phrase that said, 'called the Son of the Most High' in presenting a title for Jesus. The given statement itself embraces the concept that Jesus 'shall save his people from their sins'. This indicates that Jesus is able to exercise divine functions.

Once Mary has pronounced her vow and given her consent, then the Lord will act. The actions discussed in the annunciation scene take place and Mary then becomes pregnant and carries the future Messiah.

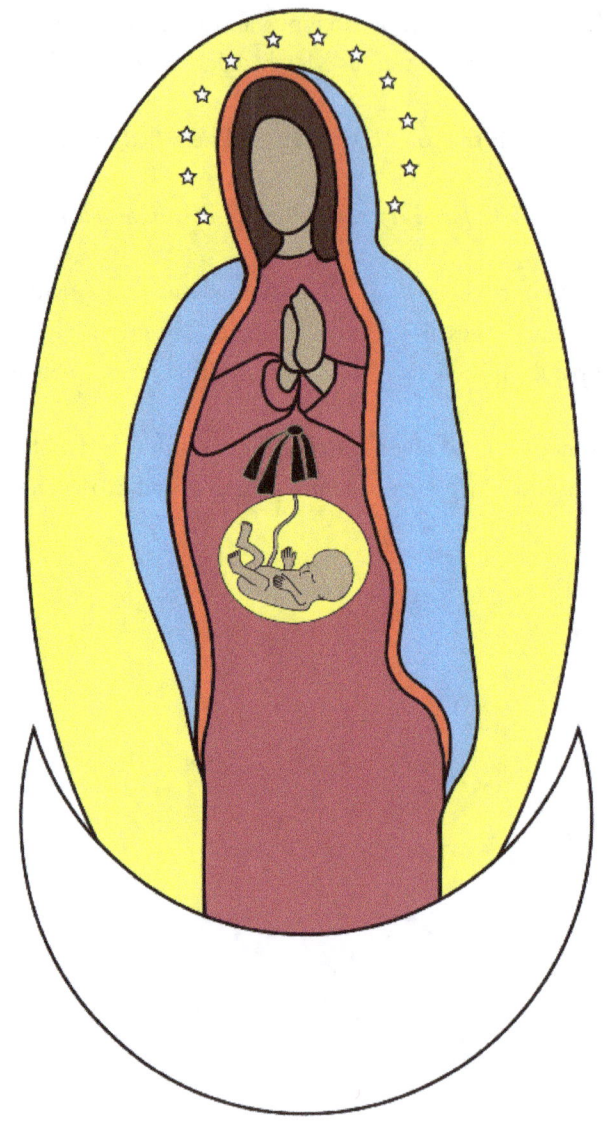

Our Lady of the Heavenly Holy of Holies

The Protevangelium of James, Chapter 12

Mary Meets the High Priest and Visits Elizabeth

12.1   And she made ready the purple and the scarlet and brought them to the high priest [Simeon]. And the high priest blessed her and said, "Mary, the Lord God has magnified your name and you shall be blessed among all generations of the earth."

12.2   And Mary, with great joy, went to Elizabeth her kinswoman and knocked on the door. When Elizabeth heard it, she put down the scarlet and ran to the door and opened it. And seeing Mary, she blessed her and said, "How is it that the mother of my Lord should come to me? For behold, that which is in me leaped and blessed you." But Mary had forgotten the mysteries that the archangel Gabriel had revealed to her and she gazed towards heaven and said, "Who am I, Lord, that all generations of the earth should bless me?"

12.3   And she remained three months with Elizabeth. And day-by-day her womb grew. And Mary was afraid and returned to her own house and hid herself from the children of Israel. And Mary was (twelve) years old when these mysterious things happened.

Commentary

12.1.a. Mary gathered her spinning of the purple and the scarlet and brought them to the high priest. The high priest blessed her and said, 'Mary, the Lord God has magnified your name and you shall be blessed among all generations of the earth'. This is very similar to the blessing that she received at the age of 3 when she was welcomed to the temple by the priest who said, 'the Lord has magnified your name in all generations. Through you, in the last days, the Lord will manifest his redemption to the children of Israel' (7.2). The high priest is aware that Mary is now pregnant, the last days are coming, and she will be blessed among all generations on earth. The original blessing was prophetic but now the prophecy has been realized and the high priest is aware of it. The watcher of Mary had heard the dialogue between the angel and Mary and had conveyed it to the high priest. The high priest is not named here but since Mary is still spinning the purple, it is not long after she came home from the temple to begin her work (10.2). The high priest is then Simeon, based on a gloss in the Syriac manuscript where it had been previously recorded as 'Samuel' (10.2.c).

12.1.b. What is surprising is left unsaid. The purple and the scarlet brought to the priest were not ritually impure. With her years of training in the temple, Mary would never have brought it back if it had been defiled. He knew that she had received a special grace from the Lord (7.3, 11.1), and in the course of nine years had always been faithful to the Lord. He recognized that Mary is not *niddah* but also that she had conceived through divine action (11.3).

The high priest was puzzled that Mary could now be pregnant if her womb was not opened , if there were no blood discharge or uterine bleeding. And this had been one of the questions that Mary had asked the angel: "Shall I conceive by the Lord, the living God?' (11.2, 11.2.b).

And he told Mary, that 'the Lord God has magnified your name' and said that 'you shall be blessed among all generations of the earth' similar to the comment of the Voice of God (11.1). Mary was startled at the blessings.

12.2.a. Then, Mary with great joy went to visit her kinswoman Elizabeth. Mary knocked on the door and when Elizabeth heard it she set down the scarlet that she was spinning and ran to the door and opened it. She was working on her own weaving, and it had nothing to do with the temple. When she saw Mary, the child in her womb had leaped and blessed Mary and she recognized that Mary carried the Lord.

The story includes a reference to the 'archangel Gabriel', not mentioned in (11.2) and (11.3) which prefer a more simple 'angel of the Lord' and this suggests that the phrase 'archangel Gabriel' may be a late import. On the other hand, Amann observes that in all the Greek texts that he has seen and the Syriac there are only insignificant variations in this material.

12.2.b. Mary also forgets things that have happened to her in (11.2) and (11.3). Amann, 1910, 228–229, regards this as a 'divine amnesia' which is a blessing for Mary since she does not have to explain what happened to her and her pregnancy. Amann notes that all the Greek manuscripts he has examined, with minor variations, and the Syriac one also, has similar text. He proposes that Mary has a spiritual suffering from this amnesia as she looks ahead to the birth of Jesus.

12.3.a. Mary remained 3 months with Elizabeth. As the days passed, her womb grew, and this frightened her. She decided to return to her house and there she hid from the children of Israel. The age that Amann attributes to Mary at the age of her conception is sixteen years although he notes that the manuscript tradition on Mary's age is inconsistent. The narrative is clear about its logical sequencing, however, and the evidence suggests that Mary's age at the time of conception is more likely to have been twelve. It is exactly this age that has discomfited commentators.

12.3.b. With respect to Mary, when she was twelve years old, there took place a council of the priests (8.2). The age of twelve is a reasonable age for Mary to be retired from her temple duties. Under divine inspiration, a call is issued to assemble the widowers of the people (8.3). Joseph, upon hearing the message, immediately went out to join them (9.1). Next, a divine prodigy points to Joseph to take into his care the virgin of the Lord (9.1). Then Joseph took her into his keeping and immediately left her in his house and went away to construct his buildings (9.3). There is no delay in the storyline regarding any of this. The narrative thrust is that Mary, who has just turned twelve, is still twelve years old.

And so, when the high priest remembered the child Mary, that she was of the tribe of David and undefiled before God they sent people to fetch her (10.1). It is significant that the text refers to the child Mary. She is still twelve years old and undefiled before God. If Mary had turned thirteen or older she would not have been considered for such work. If Mary had had her menarche in the interim, she would no longer regard herself as undefiled before God and in good conscience would have refused the summons of the high priest. When she took the scarlet and began to spin she was still twelve years old (10.2) and had not yet had her first menstruation.

The annunciation to Mary then interrupts her work on the temple veil (11.1–3). She later finishes her assignment and having made the purple and the scarlet ready she brought them to the high priest (12.1). If at any stage during this process she had shed her first menstrual blood then her work would have been defiled. Thus, the narrative itself indicates that Mary was twelve years old when she conceived Jesus and that she did so before her menarche. Jennifer Glancy,[42] who has employed a simplified version of this argument, is correct in arguing that the Protevangelium originally portrayed Mary as having conceived Jesus before her first menstruation. Nutzman, 2023:569-570, fn.38, also argues that "if Mary remains free from menstrual impurity then it is unproblematic that she continues working on the temple's curtains … even after she becomes pregnant." And this is the situation here.

From all indications in the Protevangelium, Mary's pregnancy was a normal one with the exception, as the narrative suggests, that she did not suffer from physical pain. If her pregnancy is normal then it would imply that Mary had already ovulated (or was stimulated to ovulate) when the angel spoke to her and the power of the Lord overshadowed her (11.3) and she became pregnant. Jesus is the son of Mary as well as the Son of God. If he is truly Mary's son he will have been conceived from one of Mary's eggs. Otherwise, Mary would only be a surrogate mother of Jesus.

Contrary to what many believe, it is possible to ovulate before one's first menstruation. Although unlikely, it is possible for a girl who has engaged in sexual intercourse shortly before her menarche to conceive and become pregnant, which would delay her menarche until after the delivery (Glancy, 2010, 111, fn. 109). This goes against the widely held assumption that a woman cannot become pregnant until after menarche.

---

[42] Jennifer Glancy, *Corporal Knowledge: Early Christian Bodies* (Oxford University Press, 2010), 111.

Mary's Pregnancy Discovered

13.1   And she was in her sixth month. And behold, Joseph returned from his building, and entered into his house, and found her with child. And he struck his face, and threw himself to the ground on sackcloth and wept bitterly, saying, "With what countenance shall I look upon the Lord my God? What prayer shall I offer for this girl? For I received her as a virgin out of the temple of the Lord my God and have not protected her. Who has deceived me? Who has done this evil in my house and defiled the virgin? Has the history of Adam been repeated in me? For just as Adam was in the hour of his prayer and the serpent came and found Eve alone and deceived her, so also has it happened to me.

13.2   And Joseph arose from the sackcloth and called Mary and said to her, "O you who have been so dear to God, why have you done this and forgotten the Lord your God? Why have you humiliated your soul, you who were brought up in the holy of holies and received food from the hand of an angel?"

13.3   But, she wept bitterly, saying, "I am innocent and have known no man." And Joseph said to her, "Then, from where does it come, what is in your womb?" And she said, "As the Lord my God lives, I do not know from where it comes."

Commentary

13.1.a. The preceding chapters focused on the background of Mary. Now the attention shifts to a series of hardships that Mary endures. She will suffer the suspicions not only of Joseph but also of the religious authorities. The painful scenes, however, where she will be confused, also sheds a brighter light on the holiness of Mary as well as on the supernatural character of her maternity.

The 'sixth month' can only be the sixth month of Mary's pregnancy when her condition can no longer be hidden from anyone. The annunciation to Mary took place after the departure of Joseph and the Protevangelium is precise about the chronology. The sequence of events described from (8.2) to (12.1) and (12.3.a–12.3.b) is orderly. Now that Joseph has returned after an absence of at least six months based on Mary being 12 years old at the time he left, is far more reasonable than thinking he has been away for two, three, four, or more years as some commentators have suggested (see, Hock,1995:55, n. 12:9). Any problems relating to the age of Mary are due to later copyists and not the original text.

13.1.b. The despair of Joseph is described in a picturesque manner. This prevents the reader from later fancying insulting suspicions about his interaction with Mary. Joseph threw himself to the ground on sackcloth (a fabric of coarse cloth that one wears as a sign of mourning and repentance, used here as a euphemism; see Genesis 37:34). He imagines that he has failed in his duty to protect Mary. His agony is not just that he has been deceived, but he also finds a personal fault and blames himself. He was responsible for ensuring the holiness of Mary, and now he has failed in that mission. How can he dare raise his eyes to heaven and how can he address in his prayer the virgin who had been entrusted to him by God? (Amann, 1910:231).

Having voiced his personal repentance, Joseph turns to the one he suspects is behind it all. Would this have been a new beginning of history as had once arisen from Adam? While he was praying alone, at the appropriate hour, Eve had been seduced. The serpent had not only seduced Eve in that it led her to eat the forbidden fruit; in this case, he has actively seduced her.

He does not mean, however, that this would have been so for Mary. The most natural idea is that of an ordinary seduction which is why he wants to question Mary and find from her the name of her seducer. At first, he begins to reproach her for her presumed misconduct, a fault all the more serious since her holiness was particularly sacred. (Amann, 1910:251).

13.2.a. Joseph rose from the sackcloth and called Mary. He questioned, as to how it was possible that she, who had been raised in the temple in such an extraordinary way could have forgotten the Lord, her God, like this. He asked, how was it possible that she had humiliated her soul – a Hebrew expression – when she had been 'brought up in the [heavenly] holy of holies and received food from the hand of an angel'. One may wonder how Joseph knew this, but the high priest must have informed him before he took Mary as his ward, as would be fitting. One must infer from the narrative that this was a temple secret that had been made by the priests after the events in (7.3) and (7.4).

The phrase 'brought up in the [heavenly] holy of holies and received food from the hand of an angel' has become a code phrase for the situation of Mary who has been given a unique access to God and to protection from God.

The priests now also have other secrets with respect to (11) and to (12.1) but Joseph has no information about these events.

13.3.a. Mary weeps bitterly and affirms that she is 'innocent' and has 'known no man'. And to the question of where of her pregnancy come from, she replies in her state of divine amnesia, 'As the Lord my God lives, I do not know from where it comes.'

The text is very present to the troubling effects of how the pregnancy affects both Joseph and Mary. Mary's responses are not evasive, she simply does not know what happened to her. This would be a nightmare for any woman, to find herself pregnant and not know how it happened. The entire scene is very spiritually painful to both Joseph and Mary.

The Annunciation (Joseph)

14.1   And Joseph, in great fear, parted from her, pondering what he should do with her. And Joseph said, "If I conceal her sin, I am in opposition to the law of the Lord. If I denounce her to the children of Israel, I fear that [the child] which is in her might be from an angel and I should deliver innocent blood to the judgment of death. What then shall I do with her? I will send her away secretly." And night came upon him.

14.2   And behold, an angel of the Lord appeared to him in a dream, saying, "Fear not this child for what is in her is of the holy spirit. She will bear a son, and you shall call his name Jesus; for he will save his people from their sins." And Joseph awoke from his sleep and glorified the God of Israel who had given him this grace, and he guarded her.

Commentary

14.1.a. Joseph, in great fear, parted from Mary, and pondered what to do with her. He believed that if he concealed her sin he would be in opposition to the law of the Lord. This law is likely that prescribed in Deuteronomy 22:28.

> Antiphon. If a man meets a virgin who is not engaged, and seizes her and lies with her, and they are caught in the act, the man who lay with her shall give fifty shekels of silver to the young woman's father, and she shall become his wife. Because he violated her he shall not be permitted to divorce her as long as he lives. (Deuteronomy 22:28).

14.1.b. The temple has assigned Joseph as the ward or guardian of Mary. There is no question that Mary is pregnant but, on the other hand, Joseph has been away for several months working on his buildings (9.3) and Mary has returned only recently after she is in her sixth month after being with her kinswoman Elizabeth for three months. He could not be implicated in the act. Joseph has had no contact with Mary since he first received her from the temple. She has become pregnant, and he is not the cause of it. Mary also confessed that she has known no man and has no idea of where her pregnancy came from. There is no solution because of Mary's divine amnesia.

Joseph cannot find a resolution to the situation. At the same time, he worries about the child in Mary. He feared that it might be from an angel, a popular concept at the time that likely originated from early portions of Genesis.

Antiphon. When Enoch had lived for sixty-five years, he became the father of Methusaleh. Enoch walked with God after the birth of Methusaleh for three hundred years, and had other sons and daughters. Thus all the days of Enoch were three hundred and sixty-five years. Enoch walked with God; then he was no more, because God took him. (Genesis 5:21–24).

Antiphon. When people began to multiply on the face of the ground, and daughters were born to them, the Sons of God [interpreted at the time, as angels] saw that they were fair; and they took wives for themselves of all that they chose. (Genesis 6:1–2).

Amann, 1910:233–234, observed that this notion was popularized at that time by the Book of Enoch[43].

Joseph did not want to 'deliver innocent blood to the judgment of death'. He questions himself about what to do. He now begins to think that the best option is to send Mary away secretly. And then 'night came upon him' and he fell into sleep.

14.2.a. And suddenly, an angel of the Lord appeared to him in a dream. He was told that 'he should not fear the child'. He heard the strange words, that the child 'is of the holy spirit'. The angel said: 'She will bear a son, and you shall call his name Jesus; for he will save his people from their sins.' This is also found in the words of the angel of annunication to Mary (11.2).

Antiphon. Do not cast me away from your presence, and do not take your holy spirit from me. (Psalm 51:11).

Antiphon. Who has learned your counsel, unless you have given wisdom and sent your holy spirit from on high? (Wisdom 9:17).

Joseph awoke from his sleep and 'glorified the God of Israel who had given him this grace'. With great resolution, from that time on, 'he guarded her'.

---

[43] The Book of Enoch is dated to 300–200 BCE and its most recent part to 100 BCE. It is regarded as apocryphal by most Jewish or Christian church bodies.

Joseph and Mary are Questioned

15.1   And Annas the scribe came to him and said, "Joseph, why have you not appeared in our assembly?" And Joseph said to him, "Because I was weary from my journey, and I rested the first day." And he turned and saw that Mary was pregnant.

15.2   And he went running to the high priest and said to him, "Joseph, whom you vouched for, has committed a grievous offence." And the priest said, "In what way?" And he said, "He defiled the virgin whom he received from the temple of the Lord and has secretly consummated the marriage with her and has not disclosed it to the children of Israel." And the priest answered and said, "Joseph, has done this?" And Annas the scribe said, "Send officers, and you will find the virgin pregnant." And the officers went and found it as he had said, and they brought her along with Joseph to the court.

15.3   And the high priest said, "Mary, why have you done this? And why have you humiliated your soul and forgotten the Lord your God —you who were brought up in the holy of holies and received food from the hand of an angel – and heard hymns and danced before him? Why have you done this?" And she wept bitterly, saying, "As the Lord my God lives, I am pure before him, and I know not man."

15.4   And the high priest said to Joseph, "Why have you done this?" And Joseph said, "As the Lord my God lives, I am pure concerning her." And the priest said, "Do not bear false witness, but speak the truth. You have secretly consummated the marriage with her and have not disclosed it to the children of Israel and have not bowed your head under the mighty hand that your seed might be blessed." And Joseph was silent.

Commentary

15.1.a. Amann and later commentators have assumed that in reading the Protevangelium there is a major concern about Mary's virginity and often use the word 'purity' as a modern analogue. The Protevangelium itself does not encourage this approach. Its main concern about Mary draws on the law of holiness that she has been obligated to follow all the days of her life. With respect to nazirites there is simply no regulation associated with virginity. Mary is dedicated to God and is 'holy to the Lord'. Her mission is to be a 'servant of the Lord'. When she entered the temple, the priests guided her in her new vocation. And this was the time when 'the Lord God sent his grace upon her (7.3). After she left the temple, she lived in the house of Joseph, who was away on business as he had left peremptorily and relied on Mary being placed under the protection of the Lord. Preceding her annunciation, the Voice of God gave a triple blessing to Mary 'acknowledging that she had received grace, that the Lord is with Mary, and that she is blessed 'among women' (11.1). In the annunciation event, the angel said that she would 'conceive by the Lord, the living God', Mary questioned the angel about both conceiving and giving birth (11.2). In both questions, she did not mention 'virginity' and is concerned about being *niddah* and thereby polluting the [heavenly] holy of holies by blood contamination. She also verbally accepted the invitation of the angel – and she affirmed Anna's vow – saying that she was 'the servant of the Lord – in his presence'. The whole question of virginity did not concern Mary even when she realized that she would become pregnant or give birth.

Annas the scribe came to Joseph's house and asked him why he hadn't appeared in their assembly (possibly at a synagogue) and Joseph replied that he had just returned from a journey and was recovering from it. And Annas turned and saw that Mary was pregnant.

15.2.a. Annas ran to the high priest and accused Joseph of a serious offence and explained that he had defiled a virgin from the temple of the Lord and had 'secretly consummated the marriage' without permission. The accusation is false because, although the high priest had initially intended a marriage for Mary he had suddenly changed his mind. Joseph complained about the idea because he was old, and Mary was but a child. Moreover, the high priest accepted the sign that the Lord had given indicating that Joseph should be paired with Mary. He then arranged for Joseph to be the guardian of Mary – and not be married to her. He would also be aware that Joseph had immediately gone off to work on his buildings and had left Mary alone. He listened to Annas, not correcting him on the marriage issue, for the priestly information on the matter was a secret of the priests. He sent officers out to bring Mary and Joseph to him.

15.3.a. The high priest questioned Mary about her pregnancy and appeared to be adversarial about it. He did not bring to light that he had previously known about her pregnancy. He asked about how she could humiliate her soul by what she had done and forgotten the Lord your God. He also brought up the familiar phrase about Mary – you who were brought up in the [heavenly] holy of holies and received food from the hand of an angel – indicating that this is how the priests of the temple thought of Mary. The phrase that Mary heard hymns and danced before him' surely refers to (7.4) and (7.4.c), when the Lord God sent his grace upon her, and she 'danced with her feet'. In response to the questions, Mary swears that she is pure before God and that she does not know man.

15.4.a. And then the high priest blamed Joseph for Mary's pregnancy, and Joseph swore, that he was pure concerning her. The priest persisted in challenging Joseph about bearing false witness, of speaking the truth, and of secretly consummating a marriage with Mary, of not disclosing it to Israel, and of not bowing his head under the Lord. And Joseph was silent.

Trial by Ordeal

16.1   And the high priest said, "Give up the virgin whom you received from the temple of the Lord." And Joseph burst into tears. And the priest said, "I will have you drink of the [bitter] water – the ordeal of the Lord – and he will make your sins manifest before your eyes."

16.2   And the high priest took it and made Joseph drink and sent him into the hill country. And he returned safe and sound. And he made Mary drink also and sent her into the hill country. And she [too] returned safe and sound. And all the people were astonished that there was no sign of sin in them.

16.3   And the high priest said, "If the Lord God has not made manifest your sins, neither do I judge you." And he sent them away. And Joseph took Mary and went away to his own house, rejoicing, and glorifying the God of Israel.

Commentary

16.1.a. The request by the high priest that Joseph return Mary to the temple is a vain hope. If Joseph surrendered Mary to the temple then the priests could arrange to monitor her pregnancy elsewhere, in a safe place, and would be there to teach the expected Messiah. Joseph who now takes his guardianship seriously, for he had been chosen by the Lord for this role, also knows why Mary was pregnant. He was suspicious of the high priest's offer. Joseph cried and would refuse such an offer. It was his God-given duty to remain with Mary.

His ploy failing, the high priest then decided to have both Joseph and Mary undergo a trial known as the 'ordeal of the Lord'.

16.1.b. The origin of the ordeal appears in Numbers 5:11–31. In this situation, it is only a trial concerning an unfaithful wife. Conrad E. L'Heureux describes the text as a ritual procedure that "provides the means of convicting or exculpating a wife suspected of unfaithfulness."[44] The lack of smoothness in the biblical text and the presence of repetition suggest that two originally separate rituals have been combined. One involved the drinking of the bitter waters – holy water into which dust from the ground of the temple is placed – and the other combined a grain offering with a curse. The woman was proved guilty if these procedures led to gory and disturbing effects. If she is innocent the trial will do her no harm. The practice is an example demonstrating the double standard of patriarchal societies in which a man has the right to submit his wife to a humiliating and despicable procedure while the man is left immune to any effects even if he had submitted his wife to the bitter waters out of jealousy.

[44] Conrad E. L'Heureux, "Numbers," in *The New Jerome Biblical Commentary* (Englewood Cliffs, New Jersey, 1990), 83.

Josephus discusses the ordeal of the Lord in *Antiquities*, 3.11.6, and like the biblical account it only applies to the woman.

16.1.c. In a later rabbinic text, Ishay Rosen-Zvi[45] observes that the ordeal of the Lord may be applied to both presumably guilty parties, the accused woman and her adulterer, c. 150 CE. She also notes that the ceremony described in the mishnah differs in several respects from that in Numbers and is a trial pertaining to the punishment of an adulteress. In the end, the *sotah* [the accused woman] is forbidden both to her husband and to her lover.

Antiphon. Just as the water checks her [the woman], so does the water check him [the man], as it says, "and it shall enter," "and it shall enter," (Numbers 5:22, 27). Just as she is forbidden to her husband, so she is also forbidden to the cuckolder, as it says, "is defiled", "and is defiled" (Numbers 5:27, 29). These are the words of Rabbi Akiva. Rabbi Yehoshua says, thus would Rabbi Zechariah ben HaKatzav expound. Rebbi says, two times it is said in the section: "if she is defiled," "she is defiled," one for the husband, and one for the cuckolder. (Mishnah Sotah 5:1)

16.1.d. In the Protevangelium, the trial is an innovation that applies to both Mary and Joseph and treats them equally. It no longer reflects a double standard. It is described as one that will 'make your sins manifest before your eyes'. Both situations are treated in parallel. It is a modernized application of an ancient ritual that is well suited for the purpose of the high priest.

16.2.a. The high priest took the 'bitter water' and made Joseph drink of it and sent him into the hill country. The notion of sending him into the 'hill country', in this case, somewhere outside of town, is intended to get him away from the town citizens. Amann, 1910:241, suggests that God is happy to manifest his power in private but not in public. In this part of the commentary, Amann also confesses his frustration because the Protevangelium is not behaving as he would like it to. He insists on focusing on Mary's virginity and on Joseph as being a righteous man. In doing so, he continually refuses to accept the narrative itself.

In terms of the narrative, the high priest has a good idea of what is happening, (12.1) and associated commentary. He knows what is going on. Joseph also knows what is going on (14.2), however the high priest does not know this. Mary herself knows what is going on but is confused by divine amnesia. Initially, the high priest appeared ready to sequester Mary under the control of the priests. But, Joseph, knowing what he does refuses. The high priest innovates based on an ancient ritual but applies it fairly to both Joseph and Mary. First he applies the trial to Joseph, not knowing what Joseph knows, and if sins of Joseph are revealed, then he is out of the picture. The high priest also knows that Mary will pass the test. And then the priests can take Mary back, sequester her, and guide her and the Messiah. These are all presumptions about what is happening given what the high priest knows, what Joseph knows, and what Mary knows. The Protevangelium does not discuss these matters.

16.2.b. When Joseph returns safe and sound then the high priest also made Mary drink of the 'bitter water' and sent her into the wilderness. Witnesses who see the pregnant Mary go into the wilderness fully expect that her 'sin' will be revealed, although as noted earlier, the high priest is confident that she will pass the trial.

[45] Ishay Rosen-Zvi, "Sotah, Tractate," in *Jewish Women: A Comprehensive Historical Encyclopedia* (Jewish Women's Archive, 2009).

When Mary returned safe and sound, 'all the people were astonished that there was no sign of sin in them'.

16.3.a. The high priest, who had planned for a different outcome, fully accepted the testimony of the trial. And he proclaimed, 'if the Lord God has not made manifest your sins, neither do I judge you'. Thus, both Mary and Joseph are both publicly justified in Israel and may continue their lives without harm coming to them from the community.

Joseph took Mary and then 'went away to his own house', rejoicing and glorifying the God of Israel.

16.3.b. The high priest will continue to monitor Mary, for the priests believe that she will be the mother of the Messiah.

The Road to Bethlehem

17.1 Now there came a decree from the Emperor Augustus that all the people in Bethlehem of Judea should be enrolled. And Joseph said, "I shall enroll my sons but what shall I do with this child? How am I to register her? As my wife? I am ashamed. As my daughter then? But all the children of Israel know that she is not my daughter. The day of the Lord shall be as the Lord wills."

17.2 And he saddled the ass and set her upon it; and his son led, and Joseph followed. And when they had come around the 'threemile marker' [about 4.8 km], Joseph turned and saw her sad and said to himself, "Perhaps the child within her distresses her." And again Joseph turned and saw her laughing. And he said to her, "Mary, what does it mean? – your face? – sometimes you are laughing and sometimes you are sad?" And Mary said to Joseph, "It is what I see with my eyes; two peoples – one weeping and lamenting and one rejoicing and exulting."

17.3 And having come halfway, Mary said to him, "Take me down from the ass, for the child within me presses to come forth." And he took her down from the ass and said to her, "Where shall I lead you to protect your modesty, for this place is a desert?"

Commentary

17.1.a. The chapter opens with a decree from the Emperor Augustus that all people in Bethlehem of Judea should be enrolled. There is no external evidence for such a census at this date occurring during the reign of Herod the Great. The statement is problematic.

17.1.b. Joseph muses about recording his sons. There is no mention about his daughters because they are likely married and are no longer his concern. But Mary creates a problem. He cannot refer to her as his wife for that would shame him. He cannot describe her as his daughter for the children of Israel know otherwise. He ends up by simply trusting in the Lord.

17.2.a. Joseph's little caravan proceeds with Mary seated on an ass, one of Joseph's sons leading, and Joseph at the back, behind Mary. Amann, 1910:245, goes into a lot of analysis on the trip and he argues that they reach a point about '3 miles' [4.8 km] from Bethlehem. Joseph looks at Mary and thinks that she is distressed because she looks sad. And the next time he looks, he sees her laughing. He asked Mary what was going on. He said that at times her face was laughing and at other times was sad.

17.2.b. Mary explains to Joseph, that she has an interior vision in which she sees two peoples, one weeping and lamenting and the other rejoicing and exulting.

This recalls the words the Lord spoke to Rebekah in her pregnancy. "Two nations are in your womb, and two peoples born of you shall be divided; one shall be stronger than the other, the elder shall serve the younger" (Genesis 25:23). These peoples, however, are not in Mary's womb but before her eyes, that is, she foresees that her unborn child will cause the joy of one and the sadness of the other. The feelings of the two peoples are reflected on her face. The episode is intended to show that Mary is not subject to the physical pains of maternity and that her anguish is purely spiritual. The two peoples in question are not necessarily Jews and Gentiles but rather believers and unbelievers (Amann, 1910:246). Hock, 1995:63, fn. 17:9, comes to a similar conclusion.

17.3.a. When they have come about half-way (between the three-mile marker and Bethlehem), that is, about 2.5 km from Bethlehem, Mary asked Joseph to take her down from the ass, for her child seemed ready to come. The words do not mean that she feels the pains of childbirth, only that the end of her pregnancy is near (Amann, 1910:247). Joseph took her down.

17.3.b. Joseph said to Mary, 'Where shall I lead you to protect your modesty, for this place is a desert?'. The words are sometimes translated as 'hide your shame' or 'cover your disgrace' but a more courteous description is used here (Amann, 1910:301). Hock, 1995:63, 'Where will I take you to give you some privacy?', shows a similar degree of civility.

Creation Pauses

18.1   And he found a cave there and had her enter. And leaving her in the care of his sons, he went out to seek a Hebrew midwife in the region of Bethlehem.

18.2   And I, Joseph, was walking and was not walking.
And I was looking at the sky and seeing the sky in amazement.
And I was looking at the vault of heaven and it was standing still
and the birds of the sky were not moving.
And I was looking down at the earth and a bowl was lying there.
And workmen were reclining and their hands were in the bowl.
And those that were eating were not eating.
And those that were lifting [food] were not lifting.
And those putting food in their mouth were not putting.
But the faces of all were looking upwards.
And behold, sheep were being driven and the sheep were not advancing.
And the shepherd was raising his hand to strike, and his hand was remaining up.
And I was looking at the flow of the river and was seeing the mouths of the kids
over it and they were not drinking.

18.3   Then, suddenly, everything returned to as it was.

Commentary

18.1.a. Joseph had found a cave near where they had stopped and had Mary enter into it. He left his sons nearby. Some manuscripts add "outside the cave," which seems more suitable. And then he went in search of a Hebrew midwife (Amann, 1910:247). Mary had asked the angel of annunciation about her conception and about giving birth. The angel told Mary how she would conceive (11.2), but the message itself was opaque. Yet, she did conceive and was now pregnant. The high priest who received the weaving of the scarlet and the purple from Mary in (12.1) recognized that Mary was pregnant based on the blessing that he had given her and by accepting the work of Mary, taken without concern of blood defilement because of ritual impurity in Mary.

Now, it was time to give birth and Mary had to accept in faith what the angel had told her in (11.2).

18.1.b. This is the first time that more than one of Joseph's sons are mentioned as being in the caravan. Joseph had entrusted the care of Mary to them as he went and looked for a Hebrew midwife.

Given the necessity of maintaining ritual purity, no Jewish male would have been present at the birth. Thus, Joseph's sons would naturally have remained outside the cave and no additional comment was in fact needed.

18.1.c. Throughout the gestation of Jesus, his presence in the world was cloaked in the veil of Mary's sanctuary with only two exceptions: (1) the high priest who recognized it through indirect evidence (12.1, 12.1.a, 12.1.b); (2) Elizabeth whose unborn child 'leaped and blessed' Mary at the time when Mary first visited her (12.2, 12.2.a).

The time has come for 'the Holy One to be born of you' who shall be called 'the Son of the Most High' (11.3) will be born. It is a hallowed moment when the universe paused, as if holding its breath. It is a time for a theophany that marks the entrance of Jesus into the world. (Amann, 1910:249; see also, Hock, 1995:65, fns. 18:3–11, 18:3, 18:6–7).

18.2.a. In the translation, I have taken the change to the first person as indicating that the author wished to express things differently and have interpreted this as a poetic form. The known world pauses at the birth of Jesus, and Joseph describes it. Various features indicate that Jesus was likely born in the evening, towards the end of the day: the workers are eating their meal; the sheep are returning; the kids are going to drink; and it is near sunset, the easiest time to notice the vault of heaven. (Amann, 1910:249).

The description of the workers taking their meal is picturesque. The expression that 'their hands were in the bowl' indicates that they were eating.

18.3.a. Many later manuscripts have not understood the final sentence and have omitted it or replaced it with something else. The sense is very clear in the Syriac, "And suddenly, everything was loosed and ran in order." (Amann, 1910:249).

The Birth of Jesus

19.1 And behold, a woman was coming down from the hill country.
And she said to me, "Man, where are you going?"
And I said, "I am seeking a Hebrew midwife."
And she answered me, "Are you from Israel?"
And I said to her, "Yes."
And she said, "And who is she who is bringing forth in the cave?"
And I said, "A woman betrothed to me."
And she said to me, "She is not your wife?"
And I said to her, "She is Mary, who was brought up in the temple of the Lord
    and I received her by lot as my wife.
And yet she is not my wife but has conceived of the holy spirit."
And the midwife said to him, "Is this true?"
And Joseph said to her, "Come and see."
And she went with him.

19.2 And they arrived at the place of the cave. And behold, a luminous cloud overshadowed the cave. And the midwife said, "My soul is magnified today, because my eyes have seen amazing things, salvation is born to Israel." And immediately the cloud disappeared from the cave and a great light shone in the cave so that their eyes could not bear it. And a moment later that light decreased until the infant appeared and went and took the breast of his mother Mary. And the midwife cried out and said, "This is a great day for me because I have seen this new sight."

19.3 And the midwife came out of the cave and Salome met her. And she said to her, "Salome, Salome, I have seen a new thing to tell you: a virgin has brought forth, a thing which her condition does not allow. And Salome said, "As the Lord my God lives, unless I put my finger there and test her condition I will not believe that a virgin has brought forth."

Commentary

19.1.a. The narrative continues for some time in the first person and changes suddenly in (19.2) into the third person. The mountain [translated as hill country above] may be the steep hill on which Bethlehem is situated.

A woman came down from the hill country and asked Joseph where he was going. Joseph replied that he was looking for a Hebrew midwife. Meyer, 1904, believed that the question focused on Israelite midwives because it draws attention to the Hebrew midwives whose fame had been well established.

> Antiphon. The king of Egypt said to the Hebrew midwives, one of whom was named Shiphrah and the other Puah, "When you act as midwives to the Hebrew women, and see them on the birthstool, if it is a boy, kill him; but if it is a girl, she shall live." But the midwives feared God; they did not do as the king of Egypt commanded them, but they let the boys live. So the king of Egypt summoned the midwives and said to them, "Why have you done this, and allowed the boys to live?" The midwives said to Pharaoh, "Because the Hebrew women are not like the Egyptian women; for they are vigorous and give birth before the midwife comes to them." So God dealt well with the midwives; and the people multiplied and became very strong. And because the midwives feared God, he gave them families. (Exodus 1:15–21)

19.1.b. After a basic introduction, the midwife asked Joseph, "And who is she who is bringing forth in the cave?". This is surprising since Joseph had not informed her that he had left Mary in the cave. The most likely answer is that the midwife may have been following Mary and Joseph at a distance – at the instruction of the high priest who is concerned about the birth since Mary's time is near – and at that time noticed that Mary was left in the cave.

Joseph, then revealed something of the story of Mary, including that she conceived 'of the holy spirit' (14.2). The midwife is not disturbed by this, supporting the notion that that she had been sent by the high priest who had given her some basic information about Mary and what was happening. She may have been surprised that Joseph spoke of it, because she simply asked him, "Is this true?"

Joseph told her to come and see, and she then accompanied him to the cave.

19.2.a. The text now shifts into the third person. When they (that is, Joseph and the midwife) arrive at the cave, they suddenly saw that 'a luminous cloud overshadowed the cave'.[46] Her soul is magnified by what they saw, and she professed that 'salvation is born to Israel'. This is more evidence that the high priest had informed her that there was a hope in the temple that the Messiah would soon be born, and that Mary would be the mother of the Messiah. The midwife was there to help Mary, in case she did give birth, and she did have some information about Mary. Her soul being 'magnified by what she saw' and her profession that 'salvation is born to Israel' are direct indications that she had been informed about what might happen by the priests in the temple.

Immediately, the cloud disappeared from the cave and a great light shone in the cave until their eyes could not bear it. A moment later, the light decreased 'until the infant appeared' and 'went and took the breast of his mother Mary'. The midwife had never seen such a thing, and knowing that Mary had been raised in the temple, she knew that Mary is not *niddah*. It was a great day for her, because she had never seen such a sight. The expectation that a virgin would give birth in such a way was out of this world.

[46] Hock, 1995:67, fn. 19:13, notes that the manuscripts differ over whether the cloud is 'dark' or 'bright'. The Bodmer papyrus reads 'dark cloud'. The second oldest manuscript, the Syriac, uses a term which Amann translates as 'luminous', radiant or reflecting light, such as a dark cloud with a bright light inside of it. See the continuing text which says that the 'the cloud disappeared' and 'a great light shone in the cave'.

Antiphon. Shall I open the womb and not deliver? says the Lord; shall I the one who delivers, shut the womb? says your God. (Isaiah 66:9).

Antiphon. Before she was in labour she gave birth; before her pain came upon her she delivered a son. Who has heard of such a thing? Who has seen such strange things? (Isaiah 66:7).

This antiphon essentially repeats the scene in (19.2). It is as though the midwife had seen it and reported it to the priests in Jerusalem.

Antiphon. Shall a land be born in one day? Shall a nation be born in one moment? Yet as soon as Zion was in labour she delivered her children. (Isaiah 66:8).

The language here is more symbolic, for it is Mary who represents Jerusalem (Zion) – see (4.4.b) and Isaiah 65:17–18 – and at the moment Zion (Jerusalem, Mary) was in labour, Jesus was born and the Lord 'would manifest his redemption to the children of Israel' (7.2), or, alternatively, he would 'save people from their sins' (11.3). Mary is depicted as the personification of the new Jerusalem for it is through her that the Messiah has come.

19.2.b. When Mary was born (5.2), Anna followed all of the stipulations of the law of holiness that were required by the vow that she had made. At that time, Mary was a newborn and Anna was required to follow the law of holiness. The Israelite midwife knew of such concerns.

In answer to the two questions from Mary to the angel at the annunciation (11.2), one concerned how she would conceive and the other about how she would give birth. The angel only gave one answer, 'the power of the Lord shall overshadow you'. There is no vision of the conception of Jesus, although one sees the aftermath in (12.1), (12.1a), and (12.1.b), and also in (12.2) during the visitation to Elizabeth. These both demonstrated that Mary is not *niddah* after the conception of Jesus.

Now, with the birth of Jesus, the statement 'the power of the Lord shall overshadow you' is visually portrayed. The reader is able to see what the words mean. Joseph and the midwife first saw that 'a luminous cloud overshadowed the cave'. 'And 'immediately the cloud disappeared from the cave and a great light shone in the cave so that their eyes could not bear it'.

And Jesus was born. A moment later that light decreased until the 'infant appeared and went and took the breast of his mother Mary'. The midwife cried out, "This is a great day for me because I have seen this new sight". Mary is not *niddah*.

Mary had conceived without violating the law of holiness. Mary had given birth without violating the law of holiness. The Lord had acted with power on Mary so that she would neither defile the heavenly holy of holies nor defile Jesus, the Son of the Most High, who dwelled in her. The power of the Lord had protected Mary from being *niddah* at the conception of Jesus, throughout her pregnancy, and at the birth of Jesus.

It is through the power of God that Mary was a virgin prepartum and a virgin postpartum because of the law of holiness. In good conscience, she had been concerned about the law of holiness. But the angel of annunciation urged her to trust in the power of God. Mary did so and the Lord acted.

19.2.c. It is interesting to be aware of other instances in which 'the power of the Lord' or 'the glory of the Lord' had been visible among the Israelites. One of these is Ezekiel 43:1–2, 4–5, that has been described in (7.4.b) and is a vision that Mary saw when she was about 3 years old (7.4). The appearance of the 'glory of God' that is most similar to Mary's experience in (19.2) is also found in several other episodes that are well known in Israelite history.

> Antiphon. Then Moses said to Aaron, 'Say to the whole congregation of the Israelites, "Draw near to the Lord, for he has heard your complaining." ' And as Aaron spoke to the whole congregation of the Israelites, they looked towards the wilderness, and the glory of the Lord appeared in the cloud. (Exodus 16:9–10).

> Antiphon. Then the cloud covered the tent of meeting, and the glory of the Lord filled the tabernacle, Moses was not able to enter the tent of meeting because the cloud settled upon it, and the glory of the Lord filled the tabernacle. (Exodus 40:34–35).

> Antiphon. And when the priests came out of the holy place, a cloud filled the house of the Lord, so that the priests could not stand to minister because of the cloud for the glory of the Lord filled the house of the Lord. (1 Kings 8:10–11).

> Antiphon. And it happened in the year that King Ozias died that I saw the Lord sitting on a throne, lofty and raised up, and the house was full of his glory. And seraphim stood around him; the one had six wings and the one had six wings, and with two they covered their face, and with two they covered their feet, and with two they flew. And they cried out one to another and said: "Holy, holy, holy is the Lord Sabaoth; the whole earth is full of his glory." And the lintel was raised at the voice with which they cried out, and the house was filled with smoke. (Isaiah 6:1–4, NETS).

19.3.a. The story of Salome will continue throughout chapter 20. When the midwife came out of the cave she met Salome and recognized her. It is likely that both were sent out to be of assistance to Mary who was close to term when she and Joseph headed for Bethlehem. The midwife began to tell Salome that a virgin has brought forth, a situation that her condition should not allow. However, before she can continue, Salome swears – as the Lord my God lives – that unless she puts her finger there and tests her, she will not believe that a virgin has born a child.

The narrative has already informed us of Mary's virginity, but it has been discussed within a proper context that explains how it happened. Salome now wants to demonstrate it to herself, and is determined to take direct action. It is surprising that Salome expresses no interest in the baby that was born because she had failed to listen to the midwife's tale of the birth. She is consumed by the clinical fact that a virgin had given birth.

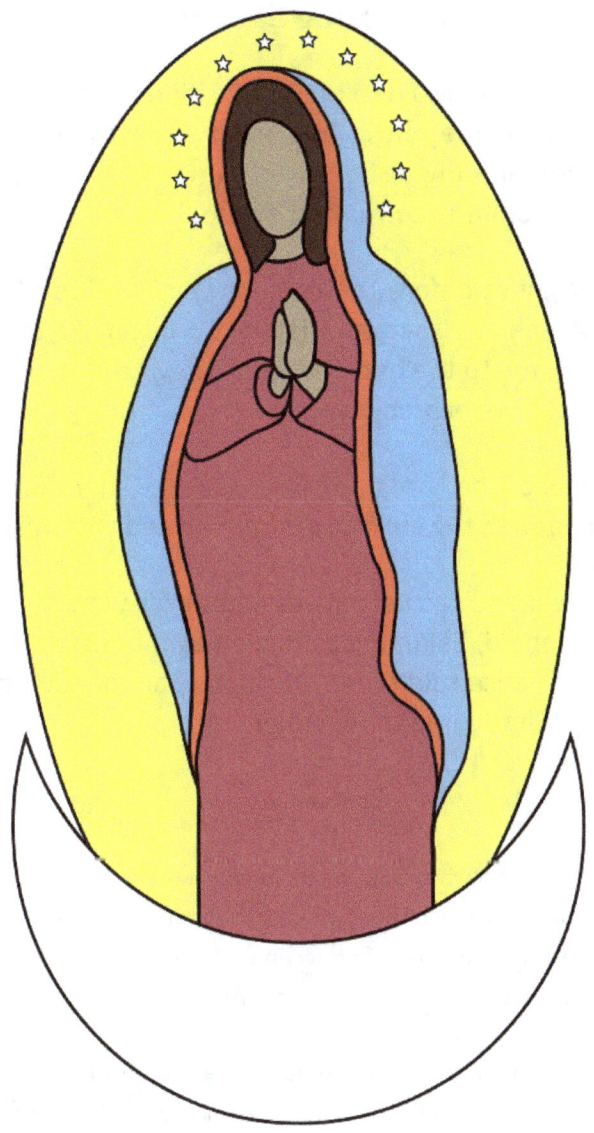

Our Lady of Jerusalem / Our Lady of Zion

Doubting Salome

20.1   And the midwife went in and said to Mary, "Position yourself, for no small controversy has arisen about you." And Salome put in her finger to test her condition, and cried out, saying, "Woe for my impiety and my disbelief, because I have tempted the living God and behold, my hand falls away from me, consumed by fire!"

20.2   And she fell on her knees before the Lord, saying, "O God of my fathers, remember me, for I am the seed of Abraham, Isaac, and Jacob. Do not make an example of me for the children of Israel but restore me to the poor. For you know, Lord, that in your name I perform my duties and from you I receive recompense."

20.3   And behold, an angel of the Lord appeared, saying to her, "Salome, Salome, the Lord has heard you. Bring your hand to the child and carry him and you will have salvation and joy."

20.4   And Salome came near and carried him, saying, "I will worship him, for a great king has been born to Israel." And behold, Salome was healed as requested and she went out of the cave justified. And behold, a Voice said to her, "Salome, Salome, do not report what marvels you have seen until the child has come to Jerusalem."

Commentary

20.1.a. The scene in this chapter is sufficiently realistic that it has startled many copyists and some variants have effectively glossed over the original text, which was deemed to be a bit crude. One must judge the whole episode not with modern ideas but according to the ideas and feelings of Salome who thought it quite natural to make note of the miracle of childbirth using both sight and touch (Amann, 1910:254-255).

The midwife and Joseph were present at the birth of Jesus. There is no evidence that anyone else witnessed it. The midwife entered the cave and Salome apparently followed her. The midwife then asked Mary to position herself because of a controversy about her. This was a 'professional action' among midwives and Mary complied. Salome put her finger to test Mary's condition and then cried out, 'Woe to my impiety and my disbelief, because I have tempted the living God and behold, my hand falls away from me, consumed by fire!'

20.1.b. Salome was 'testing Mary' and letting her finger approach her vagina and suddenly her hand fell away and began to burn. Given the narrative, Mary had given birth to the Messiah who in (11.3) was given the title 'Son of the Most High' and he has divine status. Mary is a holy of holies and Salome's finger approached the sacred space, and her finger and hand began to burn. This is the curtain sheltering her womb, a sacred place that is under the protection of God. Salome proves nothing about Mary's virginity. Her finger and hand are burning as a sign that she has attempted to defile a sanctuary.

> Antiphon. They carried the ark of God on a new cart, and brought it out of the house of Abinadab, which was on the hill. Uzzah and Ahio, the sons of Abinadab, were driving the new cart with the ark of God and Ahio went in front of the ark. David and all the house of Israel were dancing before the Lord with all their might, with songs and lyres and harps and tambourines and castanets and cymbals. When they came to the threshing floor of Nacon, Uzzah reached out his hand to the ark of God and took hold of it, for the oxen shook it. The anger of the Lord was kindled against Uzzah; and God struck him there because he had reached out his hand to the ark; and he died there before the ark of God. (2 Samuel 6:3–7).

Salome cried out, saying, "Woe for my impiety and my disbelief." She has clearly disbelieved the first midwife regarding Mary's virginity, but this is not why she is being punished. As a midwife she has a professional privilege that allows her to check on a patient after she has given birth. While her stated intention is to check Mary's virginity (19.3), there is nothing improper in her physical action. She is being punished because she has attempted to defile the sanctuary of Mary's womb.

Salome has accused herself of 'impiety' – a term rendered as 'wickedness' by Elliott, 2022, 'iniquity' byWalker,1886, and 'transgression' by Hock, 1995. The sense is that Salome has crossed the line in a religious sense. With respect to temple holiness, "the holy of holies has greater sanctity than all of these, because no one may enter there except the High Priest on the Day of Atonement" (Mishnah Kelim 1:9).

Therefore, Salome violated the law that no one must approach the holy of holies of Mary, and she suffered the consequences. Her impiety is because she tempted the living God (19.3) and is being chastised for trying to defile a sacred place.

So, what can be said of Mary's virginity? It is referred to once in the Protevangelium in a conversation between one midwife and another (19.3). This, however, proves nothing. Its reality is only proved by the scene in (19.2) when Jesus appeared and immediately took the breast of Mary, and it can only be understood through the law of holiness.

Salome attempted to verify it in (20.1) by a digital examination. This is a complete failure since her finger and hand were being burned through a divine act. There is no physical evidence of what she felt, only her burning finger and hand.

Mary's virginity can be discovered by uncovering the theological foundation laid down in the narrative. Her virgininty is an accidental quality that only surfaces after reflection on the theological program in the narrative. The burnt finger and hand of Salome do not prove anything except that she was impetuous in her investigation of Mary.

20.2.a. Salome fell on her knees before the Lord, the God of Israel, as witnessed by her prayer to the 'God of my fathers'. The focus is on her impiety and tempting the living God (20.1) and it is from him that she seeks forgiveness. She mentions her Israelite background noting that she is a descendant of Abraham, Isaac, and Jacob. She asks God not to make her an example for the children of Israel because of what she had done but to restore her to the poor. She herself is poor and performs her duties as a midwife in the name of the Lord and she does not request payment. Her only recompense is what the Lord provides. (Amann, 1910:337).

20.3.a. An angel of the Lord then appeared to Salome, calling her twice, and informs her that the Lord has heard her. The angel invites her to go to the child and carry him. It is surprising that the child has been ignored up until this moment, but the angel corrects the situation. It is by being with Jesus, in this case, by carrying him, that Salome will have 'salvation and joy'.

20.4.a. Salome accepted what the angel said and came near to Jesus and carried him. From whatever happened, her trauma with her hand at the examination, the heartfelt prayer that she had made, the Lord had heard her, or the appearance of the angel, she recognized that the child was very special. She felt a need to worship him and accepted that a great king had been born to Israel. Suddenly, she was healed as requested and she went out of the cave justified.

This was the first miracle that Jesus worked on the earth.

Suddenly, a Voice said to her, do not report what marvels you have seen until the child comes to Jerusalem. This is the 'messianic secret', first proclaimed by the Voice of God, on the day that Jesus was born. The comment when 'the child comes to Jerusalem' is a prophecy about the death of Jesus in Jerusalem. The 'messianic secret' covers the entire life of Jesus from his birth to his death.

20.4.b. Antiphons

> Antiphon. Rejoice with Jerusalem, and be glad for her, all you who love her; rejoice with her in joy, all you who mourn over her – that you may nurse and be satisfied from her consoling breast; that you may drink deeply with delight from her glorious bosom. (Isaiah 66:10–11).

> Antiphon. For thus says the Lord: I will extend prosperity to her like a river, and the wealth of the nations like an overflowing stream; and you shall nurse and be carried on her arm, and dandled on her knees. (Isaiah 66:12).

> Antiphon. As a mother comforts her child, so will I comfort you; you shall be comforted in Jerusalem. (Isaiah 66:13).

> Antiphon. Sing aloud, O daughter Zion; shout, O Israel! Rejoice and exult with all your heart, O daughter Jerusalem! The Lord has taken away the judgments against you, he has turned away your enemies. The king of Israel, the Lord, is in your midst; you shall fear disaster no more. On that day it shall be said to Jerusalem: Do not fear, O Zion; do not let your hands grow weak. The Lord, your God

is in your midst, a warrior who gives victory; he will rejoice over you with gladness, he will renew you in his love; he will exult over you with loud singing as on a day of festival. (Zephaniah 3:14 –17).

Antiphon. Take off the garment of your sorrow and affliction, O Jerusalem, and put on forever the beauty of the glory from God. Put on the robe of the righteousness that comes from God; Put on your head the diadem of the glory of the Everlasting; for God will show your splendour everywhere under heaven. For God will give you evermore the name, 'Righteous Peace, Godly Glory'. … For God will lead Israel with joy, in the light of his glory, with the mercy and righteousness that come from him. (Baruch 5:1–4, 9)

In accordance with its introduction, Baruch, Jeremiah's secretary, wrote the letter in Babylon after the deportation, and sent it to Jerusalem to be read at liturgical gatherings. The most probable date of composition is about 50 BCE (NJB, 1985;1173).

The notion that Mary is visualized as both the personified Jerusalem and as daughter Zion are derived from messianic promises in Isaiah.

Antiphon. A shoot shall come out from the stock of Jesse, and a branch shall grow out of his roots. The spirit of the Lord shall rest on him, the spirit of wisdom and understanding, the spirit of counsel and might, the spirit of knowledge and the fear of the Lord. (Isaiah 11:1–2).

Antiphon. The Lord has proclaimed to the ends of the earth: Say to daughter Zion, 'See your salvation comes; his reward is with him, and his recompense before him. They shall be called, The Holy People, The redeemed of the Lord'; and you shall be called, 'Sought Out, A City Not Forsaken.' (Isaiah 62:11–12).

Isaiah 65–66 are prophecies that recognize the coming of Mary and the coming of Jesus as the Messsiah. The documentation is present in the interlocking references between the prophecies and the Protevangelium itself.

The first such notice is from Isaiah 65:17–18 which begins with the conception of a child that is predicted in (4.1) and which occurs following (4.4). God's plans are about to be revealed and 'new heavens and a new earth' are going to be created and God will create 'Jerusalem as a joy' and its 'people as a delight'.

At this point we have the prophecy but do not know how it will unfold. What we know is based on the vow of Anna, her child will be a nazirite dedicated to the Lord for all the days of its life and shall be a 'servant of the Lord'. The angel of annunciation says to Anna that her offspring 'shall be known throughout the world'. This will begin following Mary's conception in (4.1). Anna must follow the 'law of holiness' as applied to the priests of the temple and this will occur even before her child is born.

Following the birth of her child, she is named 'Mary', and Anna must continue to follow the law of holiness and Anna does so immediately by imposing the necessary holiness legislation upon herself for the sake of Mary (5.2).

As a nazirite, Mary has been registered at the temple, however, as an infant she is left in the care of Anna. At the age of six months, Anna must build a sanctuary for Mary. The temple provided 'undefiled daughters of the Hebrews' to visit her and entertain Mary (6.1). At the same time, the temple is aware of Mary and are taking her seriously.

At the age of one year, Joachim prepared a feast, not because of her birthday, but as an occasion to introduce Mary to the priests of the temple. The priests give Mary a blessing while the high priests give Mary a messianic blessing. In (6.3) Anna sings a song to the Lord showing a connection with Rachel, the mother of Joseph, and matriarch of David from whom shall come the Messiah. Matrilineal descent is being suggested and Anna's song becomes messianic according to the traditions of Isaiah.

 At three years of age, Mary is weaned, and is brought to the temple, where she is welcomed by a priest (possibly the high priest). At this point, she is welcomed by a messianic blessing that the Lord has magnified her 'name in all generations' and that 'in the last days, 'the Lord will manifest his redemption to the children of Israel' (7.2). The priests are heavily involved in guiding Mary.

Mary then has a prophetic encounter with the Lord associated with Ezekiel's prophecy of a New Temple in which 'the Lord God sent his grace upon her' and in some sense she is the holy of holies in the heavenly temple although she remains on earth as a three-year-old girl living in the temple who is holy to the Lord (7.3). In terms of the texts of Ezekiel, she appears as a representative of a new Jerusalem, through whom the Messiah will be born, and as mother of the messianic age that will begin with an outpouring of water (the well of salvation) that will pour out from the east wall of the temple and overflow the earth. Related concepts are found in various texts such as Isaiah 65:17–19 used after (4.4) dealing with the conception of Mary.

The narrative flow of the Protevangelium is sufficiently discussed in detail in the preceding chapter commentaries and will not be repeated here.

At this point, some prophecies from the Old Testament will cease for they will be completed only in the age of the New Testament. The Protevangelium is not in the New Testament and the only references being used to analyze its text are from the Old Testament. If we continue with these prophecies one is entering into the age of the New Testament. We are at the borderline between the two and it is time to pause.

The Journey of the Magi

21.1   And behold, Joseph was ready to go into Judea. And there was a great commotion in Bethlehem of Judea. For there came magi saying, "Where is he that is born king of the Jews? For we have seen his star in the east and have come to worship him."

21.2   And when Herod heard this he was troubled and sent officers to the magi, and summoned the chief priests and questioned them, saying, "What is written concerning the Messiah? Where is he to be born?" And they said to him, "In Bethlehem of Judea, for so it is written." And he sent them away. And he questioned the magi, saying to them, "What sign have you seen concerning the newborn king?" And the magi said, "We have seen a star of great size, shining among those stars and obscuring them so that they appeared no more and so we knew that a king was born to Israel, and we have come to worship him." And Herod said, "Go and seek him and when you have found him let me know so that I may also go and worship him."

21.3   And the magi went out. And behold, the star, which they had seen in the east, went before them until they came to the cave. And it stood over the top of the cave. And the magi saw the infant with his mother Mary, and they took gifts out of their bag– gold, and frankincense, and myrrh.

21.4   And having been warned by the angel not to go into Judea, they went to their own country by another route.

Commentary

21.1.a The chapter opens with a problem because it says that 'Joseph was ready to go into Judea', but in the following sentence, it speaks of 'a great commotion in Bethlehem of Judea. In the previous episode, Joseph is in a cave adjacent to Bethlehem and is nearby. The error is transparent, and the most obvious trip for Joseph is to return to his home in Jerusalem. The first 'Judea' may be a simple copy error or a symbol for 'Jerusalem'. Joseph knows where he is because he had just voyaged from Jerusalem and stopped at the cave outside of Bethlehem just before Mary was about to give birth. There is a problem with commentators who are convinced that Joseph lived in Nazareth because of the future Gospel of Luke which, in the present historiography, would not be written for another 80 years.

21.1.b. The commotion in Bethlehem was because magi had arrived and were looking for the person who was born 'king of the Jews'. They had seen a star in the east, which had led them to Bethlehem, and they had decided to come there to worship him.

> Amann, 1910:352, recognizes that the number of the magi, their names, and their quality as kings are not mentioned because he accepts that the Protevangelium is more ancient than later developments that provide such information. He likely does not believe that such details are factual and recognizes them as popular and imaginative expositions of things that one does not know.

21.2.a. When Herod heard about the excitement in Bethlehem he was troubled and sent officers to the magi (to bring them to him). Herod summoned the chief priests and asked them about the Messiah. What is written about him and where is he to be born? They replied that it is written, 'In Bethlehem of Judea'. And then they were sent away.

When the magi arrived, he asked them about what sign they had seen concerning the newborn king. The magi responded, We have seen a star of great size, shining in the heavens and obscuring the other stars in the sky and they knew that a king was born to Israel, and they had come to worship him. And Herod sent them off to find him. He asked them to let him know where he was so that he too might go and worship him.

> Antiphon. The oracle of Balaam son of Beor, the oracle of the man whose eye is clear, the oracle of one who hears the words of God, and knows the knowledge of the Most High, who sees the vision of the Almighty, who falls down, but with his eyes uncovered: I see him but not now; I behold him but not near – a star shall come out of Jacob, and a sceptre shall rise out of Israel. (Numbers 24: 15–17).

21.3.a The magi left, and suddenly, the star which they had seen in the east, 'went before them until they came to the cave' and 'it stood over the top of the cave'. The magi then saw 'the infant with his mother Mary'. They then took presents out of their bag, gifts of gold, frankincense, and myrrh. The bag would be a leather bag into which people would squeeze all the objects necessary for a trip.

> Antiphon. A bright light will shine to all ends of the earth; many nations will come to you from far away, the inhabitants of the remotest parts of the earth to your holy name, bearing gifts in their hands for the King of Heaven. Generation after generation will give joyful praise in you; the name of the chosen city will endure forever. (Tobit 13:11)

21.4.a. An angel of the Lord warned the magi not to go into Judea (see also 21.1.a) suggesting as proposed earlier that the term Judea refers to Jerusalem and its immediate environs (Amann, 1910:261). They then decided to return to their own country by another route.

21.4.b. It is significant that Papyrus Bodmer V, the oldest manuscript of the Protevangelium in existence, abbreviates this chapter considerably (Elliott, 2006, 98, fn. 1). The present chapter, as for all the chapters, follows the Syriac manuscript which is the second oldest manuscript, and is preferred.

Jesus and John Saved from Herod

22.1 And when Herod realized that he had been deceived by the magi, he was furious and sent murderers, saying to them, "Kill the children two years old and under."

22.2 And Mary, having heard that the children were being killed, was afraid and took the child and wrapped him in swaddling clothes and laid him in an oxmanger.

22.3 And Elizabeth, having heard that they were searching for John, took him and went up into the hill country. And she was looking for somewhere to conceal him and there was no hiding place. And Elizabeth, groaning aloud, said, "O mountain of God, receive a mother with her child," for Elizabeth could not climb. And immediately the mountain was rent and received her. And a light was shining for them because an angel of the Lord was with them and protected them.

Commentary

22.1.a. When Herod saw that he had been tricked by the magi, he was infuriated. He sent murderers and killed all the children in and around Bethlehem who were two years old and under.

22.2.a. Mary, having heard that the children were being killed, was afraid. She took Jesus, wrapped him in swaddling clothes, and laid him in an ox-manger.

The information in this chapter are scattered pieces of information that the Protevangelium had access to and did not wish to leave out.

22.3.a. Elizabeth, having heard that they were searching for John, took him and escaped to the hill country. She was looking for somewhere to conceal him but could find no hiding place. She came to a mountain and, groaning, prayed, 'O mountain of God, receive a mother with her child,' and at this point in her flight, she could no longer climb.

Immediately, the mountain was rent and received her. And a light was shining for them because an angel of the Lord was with them and protected them.

22.3.b. This type of miracle is unusual in the Protevangelium and recalls various events in the apocrypha of the Old Testament. In particular it has some similarity to a cedar that opens and gives asylum to Isaiah (Amann, 1910:263).

Miracles do occur in the Protevangelium, but they are theological ones worked to bring about God's plan in salvation history. The type of 'fantastic' miracle like this one is a sign that it comes from elsewhere. In this miraculous refuge of Elizabeth and John, the mother and child do not remain in darkness, since light is able to reach them. The light does not seem to be due to the presence of the angel, in the sense that it would be the angel who emits it around himself. Rather, it seems that through the good offices of the angel, the mountain is able to allow in whatever light is needed. The text assumes that the fugitives will stay for some time in the refuge although there is no indication of how long they lived there or when they will leave (Amann, 1910, 263).

The Murder of Zechariah

23.1   And Herod was searching for John and sent officers to Zechariah, saying, "Where have you hidden your son?" And he answered and said to them, "I am the servant of God and I serve constantly in the temple of the Lord. I do not know where my son is."

23.2   And the officers departed and told all this to Herod. And Herod was enraged and said, "His son will one day be king over Israel!" And he sent [a threat] to him again, saying, "Tell the truth. Where is your son? You know that your life is in my hands." And the officers departed and told him these things.

23.3   And Zechariah said, "I am a martyr of God if you shed my blood, for the Lord will receive my spirit   because you spill innocent blood in the vestibule of the temple of the Lord. And about daybreak Zechariah was slain. And the children of Israel did not know that he had been murdered.

Commentary

23.1.a. The Protevangelium appears to assume that John the Baptist was born in Bethlehem. Herod, who knows this, and has learned of other wonders that surrounded the birth of the child, is able to see him, plausibly, as the king who was sought by the magi. Therefore, Herod asked John's father about him. Zechariah is a high priest as shown by the fact that in the following chapter the priests come in the morning to greet him. Zechariah, who stays constantly in the temple of the Lord, is able to truthfully answer that he does not know where his son is (Amann, 1910:264).

23.2.a. The officers departed and Zechariah's reply was given to Herod, and it appeared to have strengthened his suspicions. He was enraged and said, "His son will one day be king over Israel!" Then, he sent a threat to Zechariah. He must tell the truth about his son, otherwise his life as in Herod's hands. The officers departed and told Zechariah about these things.

23.3.a. Zechariah answered those who threatened him by telling them that he would be a martyr if they shed his blood, and the Lord would receive his spirit because they would spill innocent blood in the vestibule of the temple of the Lord'.

The text is difficult to establish, and the meanings fall into two groups. In the first, the order of ideas is, "God is my witness that I tell the truth, if despite this you intend to kill me, you are shedding innocent blood and so

God will receive my spirit." This is the most natural order. In the second, the meaning is, "I am not afraid of death because I am innocent." According to most manuscripts, Zechariah himself mentions 'the vestibule of the temple of the Lord' as the scene of his death. (Amann, 1910: 265).

23.3.b. The text indicates that Zechariah was murdered around daybreak. It was done secretly, because the children of Israel 'did not know that he had been murdered'.

Zechariah's Death Discovered

24.1   But at the hour of the salutation, the priests were departing, and the customary blessing of Zechariah did not take place. And the priests stood waiting for Zechariah, to greet him at the prayer and to glorify the Most High.

24.2   And when he failed to come out, they were all afraid. And one of them took courage and went in and he saw clotted blood beside the altar. And he heard a voice, saying, "Zechariah has been slain and his blood shall not be wiped away until his avenger comes." And, having heard these words, he was afraid and went out and told it to the priests.

24.3   And they took courage and entered and saw what had happened. And the ceiling panels of the temple wailed, and they rent their clothes from the top to the bottom. And they did not find his body but found his blood become like stone. And they were afraid and went out and told all the people that Zechariah had been murdered. And all the tribes of the people heard, and they mourned him and lamented three days and three nights.

24.4   And after the three days, the priests took counsel as to whom they should put in his place and the lot fell to Simeon. It was he to whom it was revealed by the holy spirit that he should not see death until he had seen the Messiah in the flesh.

Commentary

24.1.a. When the priests arrived at the temple for the greeting after the morning sacrifice, it appears that they would receive a customary blessing from the high priest, Zechariah. Then they would be off to do their duties. However, Zechariah had not shown up for they were waiting to greet him at the prayer and to glorify the Most High.

24.2.a. When Zechariah did not come out from the sanctuary, they became afraid. One of the braver priests went to look in and he saw clotted blood beside the altar. Then he heard a voice saying that Zechariah had been slain and his blood shall not be wiped away until his avenger comes. This frightened the priest, and he went out and told it to the other priests.

The clotting in question is not natural. The Syriac version already states that at this spot the blood has become like stone. The voice that is heard indicates the meaning of the prodigy. The hardened blood will remain there until the day when the avenger of Zechariah comes (Amann, 1910:267).

24.2.b. The story of Zechariah leaves no question about the murderer; it is Herod. In addition, the location of the murder also pollutes the temple, which is all the more heinous on that account. The 'avenger of blood' is significant because the clotted blood of Zechariah that has become like stone in the sanctuary and is pursuant to the angel's remark.

In general, the avenger of blood is God himself.

> Antiphon. Sing praises to the Lord, who dwells in Zion. Declare his deeds among the people. For he who avenges blood is mindful of them; he does not forget the cry of the afflicted. (Psalm 9:11–12).

In this regard, the death of Herod is particularly gruesome.[47]

24.3.a. When the priests, at the call of their colleague, enter into the sanctuary, there occurs a prodigy analogous to that of the voice heard earlier. This time, it is the panels of the temple that produce an extended wailing and the priests themselves 'tore their clothes from the top to the bottom' in a sign of mourning'. The wailing of the temple panels and the tearing of the clothes of the priests are synonymous and this indicates the symbol of the prodigy. The details are indicated in the Syriac version, and this is likely the original meaning (Amann, 1910:269).

24.3.b. The priests did not find Zechariah's body but only his blood that had 'become like stone'. The priests were fearful and went out and told all the people that Zechariah had been murdered. And all the people that heard of it mourned him and lamented three days and three nights. This mourning would also include the fact that the temple had been defiled.

The mourning of Israel recalls the general mourning in messianic prophecies made by Zechariah'sm namesake.

> Antiphon. And I will pour out a spirit of compassion and supplication on the House of David and the inhabitants of Jerusalem, so that, when they look on the one whom they have pierced, they shall mourn for him, as one mourns for an only child and weep bitterly over him, as one weeps over a firstborn. (Zechariah 12:10).

24.4.a. After three days of mourning for Zechariah, the priests took counsel as to whom they should put in his place. After making a choice by lot, it fell to Simeon. Amann, 1910:269-272, then observes that a gloss has been inserted in 10.2 in the Syriac version indicating that 'Samuel' who replaced Zechariah when he was previously mute is in fact 'Simeon' and it should be read that way.

And it was to Simeon that the holy spirit revealed to him that he would not die until he had seen the Messiah in the flesh.

---

[47] 'Researchers Diagnose Herod the Great – ABC News' (retrieved 2024.11.06)

The Author of the Protevangelium

25.1   And I, James, wrote this history in Jerusalem – as a tumult arose on the death of Herod – and withdrew into the desert until the tumult in Jerusalem ceased, praising the Lord God who had given me the gift and wisdom to write this history.

25.2   And grace shall be with all those who fear our Lord Jesus Christ, to whom be glory forever and ever. Amen.

Commentary

As is common in many early writings, the name of the author is given as a sign of the authenticity of the work. In the present case, it is James, the brother of the Lord, and the head of the Jerusalem Church. This claim is not accepted because of the messianic secret first proclaimed by the Voice of God in the Protevangelium to Salome on the day that Jesus was born (20.4.a). It would then endure until 'the child comes to Jerusalem', a prophecy of the death of Jesus in Jerusalem. The secret covers the entire life of Jesus from his birth to his death.

It has been argued that the author of the Protevangelium is ultimately the testimony of Mary, the mother of Jesus. I estimate that the original version was published in Greek, c. 35–40 CE, in the Syriac area (possibly in Antioch). The details of the transmission history from Mary to Antioch and then back to Israel remain to be investigated.

REFERENCES

NETS   A New English Translation of the Septuagint, 2007, Oxford University Press.

NJB   The New Jerusalem Bible, 1985, Doubleday.

NRSV   Holy Bible, New Revised Standard Version, Catholic Edition, *Anglicized Text*, 2007, Harper Collins Publishers.

'Researchers Diagnose Herod the Great – ABC News' (retrieved 2024.11.06)

Amann, Emile. *Le Protévangile de Jacques et Ses Remaniements Latins*. Letouzey et Ané, Editeurs, 76 Bis, Rue des Saints-Pères, Paris, 1910.

Baden, Joel S. "The Nature of Barrenness in the Hebrew Bible," in *Disability Studies and Biblical Literature*, eds. Candida R. Moss and Jeremy Schipper (pp. 13–27). Palgrave Macmillan, 2011.

Braude, W. G. (translator) *Pesikta Rabbati* (Discourses for Feasts, Fasts, and Special Sabbaths). New Haven and London: Yale University Press, 1968.

Clifford, Richard J. and Roland E. Murphy, "Exodus," Contribution No. 3 (pp. 44–60), in *The New Jerome Biblical Commentary*. Englewood Cliffs, New Jersey, 1990.

Closs, Michael P. *The Book of Mary, A Commentary on the Protevangelium of James*. FriesenPress, Victoria, BC, 2016.

Closs, Michael P. The Book of Mary, *A Commentary on the Protevangelium of James*. Second Edition. ARPress, 2025.

Conrady, L. *Die Quelle der kanonischen Kindheitsgeschichte de Jesus*. Göttingen, 1900.

Cullmann, O. "Kindheitsevangelien," in E. Hennecke, *Neutestamentliche Apokryphen in deutscher Übersetzung*. 4. Aufl. Hrsg. Von W. Schneemelcher. Mohr, Tübingen, 1968.

de Strycker, Émile. *La forme la plus ancienne du Protévangile de Jacques*. Brussels, 1961.

Elliott, J. K. *The Apocryphal New Testament: A Collection of Apocryphal Christian literature in an* English Translation Based on M. R. James. The Oxford University Press, 1993.

Elliott, J. K. *A Synopsis of the Apocryphal Nativity and Infancy Narratives*. Brill, Leiden, 2006.

Epstein, J. N. "Some Variae Lectiones in the Yerushalmi I: The Leiden MS" [Hebr.]. *Tarbiz* 5 (1933–34) 257–72.

Fabricius, J. A. *Codex apocryphus Novi Testamenti*, Hamburg, 1703; 2nd edition, 1719.

Flash-Luzzatti, S.; Weil, C.; Shalev, V.; Oron, T.; Chodick, G. "Long-term secular trends in the age at menarche in Israel: a systematic literature review and pooled analysis." Epub Feb 5, 2014.

Glancy, Jennifer A. *Corporal Knowledge: Early Christian Bodies*. Oxford University Press, 2010.

Hock, Ronald F. *The Infancy Gospels of James and Thomas*. Santa Rosa, California, 1995.

Hofmann, *Das Leben Jesu nach den Apokryphen im Zusammenhange aus den Quellen erz.hlt und wissenschaftlich untersucht*. Leipzig, 1851.

Ilan, Tal. *Mine & Yours are Hers, Retrieving Women's History from Rabbinic Literature*. Brill: Leiden, 1997.

James, M. R. *The Apocryphal New Testament*. Oxford University Press, 1924.

L'Heureux, Conrad E. "Numbers," Contribution No. 5 (pp. 80–93) in *The New Jerome Biblical Commentary*. Englewood Cliffs, New Jersey, 1990.

Levine, Baruch A. *Numbers 1-20: A New Translation with Introduction and Commentary*, AB 4A. New York: Doubleday, 1980.

Lieberman, Saul. *Hellenism in Jewish Palestine*. New York, 1950.

Manns, Frédéric. Essais sur le judéo-christianisme. Jerusalem: Franciscan Printing Press, 1977.

Marx, Dalia. *Tractates Tamid, Middot and Qinnim: A Feminist Commentary*. Mohr Siebeck, Tübingen, Germany, 2013.

Meacham (leBeit Yoreh), Tirzah. "Female Purity (Niddah)." *Jewish Women: A Comprehensive Historical Encyclopedia. 1 March 2009. Jewish Women's Archive.* (Viewed on July 31, 2015) <http://jwa.org/encyclopedia/article/ female-purity-niddah>.

Meyer, A. Commentary in Hennecke, *Neutestamentliche Apokryphen in Deutscher Uebersetzung und mit Einleitungen*. Tubingue and Leipzig, 1904.

Nutzman, Megan. "Mary in the *Protevangelium of James:* A Jewish Woman in the Temple?" *Greek, Roman, and Byzantine Studies* 53 (pp. 551–578), 2013.

Rosen-Zvi, Ishay. "Sotah, Tractate." *Jewish Women: A Comprehensive Historical Encyclopedia*. 1 March 2009. Jewish Women's Archive. (Viewed on May 27, 2015) <http://jwa.org/encyclopedia/article/sotah-tractate>.

Smid, H. R. *Protevangelium Jacobi: A Commentary*. Assen, 1965.

Tischendorf. *Evangelia Apocrypha*. Leipzig, 1876.

Walker, Alexander. (translator) "The Protevangelium of James" (pp. 351, 361–367) in *The Ante-Nicene Fathers*, vol. 8 (American Edition). Edinburgh: T&T Clark, 1886. (Revised and edited for New Advent by Kevin Knight.)

Wrede, William. Das Messiasgeheimnis in den Evangelium: *Zugleich ein Beitrag zum Verständis des Markusevangelium*. Göttingen: Vandenhoeck & Ruprecht, 1901; English edition, *William Wrede, The Messianic Secret*. Trans. The Rev'd James C. G. Grieg. Cambridge: James Clarke & Co., 1971). See also, Wikipedia, 'messianic secret'.

Zacharias, Leona and Wurtman, Richard J. "Age at Menarche: Genetic and Environmental Influences," *New England Journal of Medicine* (April 17), 280, 1969:868–875.

Zervos, George Themelios. *The Protevangelium of James, Greek text, English Translation, Critical Introduction, Volume 1*. T & T Clark, Bloomsbury Publishing, 2019 (paperback edition, 2021).